THE ARTISANAL KITCHEN

JEWISH
HOLIDAY
BAKING

Also in the Artisanal Kitchen series

THE ARTISANAL KITCHEN

JEWISH HOLIDAY BAKING

INSPIRED RECIPES FOR ROSH HASHANAH, HANUKKAH, PURIM, PASSOVER, AND MORE

Uri Scheft

with Raquel Pelzel

Artisan | New York

CONTENTS

SWEET 51

INTRODUCTION

Baked goods made from scratch are beautiful and nourishing; they have the ability to bring people together around a table or even at a kitchen counter. Baking is also a special way to mark the holidays, whether you're gathering with a houseful of family and friends or celebrating with a small group or your local community.

This collection of foolproof baking recipes, divided into savory and sweet sections, offers you delicious breads and treats for the calendar year of Jewish holidays. There is something here for every table, every palate, and every season. You'll learn how to make Poppy Seed Hamantaschen for Purim, flour-free Coconut Macaroons for Passover, Crazy and Festive Challah for Rosh Hashanah, Jachnun for a Sabbath lunch, and other decadent and inspired recipes.

Challah is, at its essence, a bread meant for social occasions: religious events, holidays, weddings, and celebrations. It holds a distinct place on the holiday table. It is also the bread served on the dinner table for Shabbat. The person seated at the head of the table says a blessing over the bread before ripping it by hand and passing each person their own piece. Made with what were once considered expensive ingredients like eggs and sugar, challah is a lightly sweet and very tender bread that pulls apart into long cottony strands. The way challah is shaped makes it special too. It is no ordinary loaf or boule: the dough is braided. Once you master a simple challah braid, you can break with tradition and play with the wide variety of shapes that can be made from this forgiving and easy-to-work-with dough.

In both content and shape, hamantaschen is also steeped in traditions that add to its holiday charm. Typically filled with poppy seeds (a classic ingredient for Purim) and formed like a tricornered hat (the symbolism of which is heavily debated—Haman's hat, the three "fathers" of Judaism, etc.), these versatile cookies lend themselves to countless variations. Once you are comfortable with the shaping of the delicate triangle, the filling possibilities are endless. Try recipes for both sweet (poppy seed or charoset) and savory (potato or beet) hamantaschen, but also have fun coming up with new combinations and finishing techniques for the cookies, such as mixing an apple filling with poppy seed filling or drizzling the baked and cooled sweet hamantaschen with melted chocolate.

Whether you're a seasoned baker or not, whether you are Jewish or not, you will be able to create these delicious holiday treats with confidence. Make no mistake: baking is a labor of love. But the options are infinite and aspirational once you get the hang of the classic recipes. For example, once you learn how to make basic babka, you can tackle unique recipes with traditional ingredients, like Apple Babka and Poppy Seed Babka. And the challah recipe, while delicious on its own, can be modified with limitless ingredients—from chocolate and candied orange peel to nuts, seeds, herbs, and marzipan. Challah can be a canvas for expressing your creativity.

Many of the bread recipes make multiple loaves, allowing you to freeze one or two to be enjoyed at a later date or to share with your friends and family at your next holiday gathering. The pastry and cookie recipes—from Sufganiyot bursting with strawberry jam, chocolate or vanilla cream, or your favorite doughnut filling to Chocolate Rugelach with its to-die-for Nutella spread—are perfect for parties and gatherings as well, as they make enough for all to enjoy. You will be everyone's favorite guest or host with these goodies in hand.

Coming together around the holiday table builds deep bonds, and the recipes here are meant to inspire you to get into the kitchen and break bread with loved ones, to continue with the old ways and create new ones, too.

A FEW NOTES, TIPS, AND TRICKS

These insider tips will help as you follow the recipes in this book.

BATCH SIZE AND INCREASING/DECREASING BATCHES LIKE A BAKER

You'll notice that many of the recipes yield multiple loaves or dozens of cookies. When making dough in a stand mixer, small amounts of ingredients don't get handled as efficiently as larger amounts. So for the best results, make the breads and other recipes as described and share them with your family and friends or freeze some for later.

If you need to increase a batch of dough, use the weight of the flour in the recipe as your 100% benchmark. So if a recipe calls for 800 grams of flour and you want to increase it to an even, simple 1 kilo (1,000 grams), multiply the amount you want to increase it to (1,000 grams) by 100, to yield 100,000. Then divide 100,000 by 800 grams (the original amount of flour, your 100% benchmark) to get 125. Finally, divide 125 by 100 to get 1.25—multiply all ingredients by 1.25 to get the new measurements. For example, if the recipe originally called for 25 grams of yeast, you multiply 25 grams by 1.25 to get 31.25 grams, which is the new amount of yeast (in grams) that you need to use in the enlarged recipe.

CALCULATION
based on 800 grams flour (100%)

---

800 grams = original amount
1,000 grams = amount you want to increase to
100 × **1,000** = 100,000 ÷ **800** = 125
125 ÷ 100 = **1.25**

multiply all ingredient quantities by 1.25
to get new amounts

BEFORE YOU BEGIN: READ, WEIGH, PREPARE

Read the recipe before you begin. Read the ingredients list, read the instructions, weigh all your ingredients, and get everything in order so you can follow the recipe exactly. Use a digital scale because it is more accurate than cup measures, meaning that your dough will be consistent from batch to batch.

You should also have all of your refrigerated ingredients at room temperature before beginning—room-temperature eggs beat with more volume; room-temperature butter creams more easily. For butter, you can microwave it in 10-second increments, checking it often, until it isn't cold but hasn't started to soften too much and become greasy.

WORK CLEAN

Invest in a bench scraper or dough scraper (see page 11) to remove excess flour and bits of dough from your work surface before sponging it off. If you start with a wet sponge, you'll end up with a floury, pasty mess. Have a trash bag handy next to the counter or in the sink, or use a large bowl that you can wipe the garbage into. Keep everything clean and organized while you work.

FLOUR: SIFTING

When flour is oxygenated, it allows for better gluten development, and the gluten can trap more air in the loaf. Sifting flour can increase a loaf of bread's volume by 10 to 15%.

FLOUR: CONVERTING ALL-PURPOSE TO WHOLE WHEAT

You can substitute up to 50% of the white flour in a recipe with whole wheat or spelt flour. You will have to add about 50 grams (3 tablespoons plus 1 teaspoon) more water to the dough to account for the heartier flour.

DON'T BE SHY WITH THE ADD-INS

A general rule of thumb when adding chocolate, seeds, nuts, dried fruits, or grains to bread is to weigh the dough, then add 20% of the weight in extra goodies. Now, for some goodies, you will need to add extra water to account for the absorbent properties of the add-ins—this is true for ingredients like quinoa and flaxseeds. Other extras, like sautéed onion and olives, actually add moisture to the dough, so you might need to reduce some liquid in the recipe. This is definitely a key point to consider when mixing the dough. In addition, always make sure you get all the extra ingredients out of the bowl or measuring cup. What is left in the cup could be 10% of the volume—the goodies really do matter! Get it all in there!

STORING AND FREEZING BREAD

When storing bread, place it in a plastic bag and fold the open end under. If the bread has already been sliced, wrap the cut end in plastic wrap and then place the whole loaf in a plastic bag. To freeze bread, wrap the loaf in two layers of plastic wrap, then in a layer of aluminum foil. To defrost frozen bread, leave the loaf out at room temperature; when it has thawed, remove the foil and plastic wrap and rewrap the loaf in foil. If you don't have time to defrost the bread first, remove the plastic wrap and foil layers from the loaf, rewrap the loaf with just the foil, and place the foil-wrapped loaf in a warm oven for 8 to 10 minutes, removing the foil for the last minute or two to crisp the crust.

THE BAKER'S TOOLKIT

The only must-haves for making bread, cookies, and other baked goods are your hands, a digital scale, and an oven. That said, here are some tools that make the process of baking cleaner, simpler, and easier.

BENCH SCRAPER

A bench scraper is a rectangular piece of metal attached to a wooden or plastic handle. When you scrape your work surface (which bakers call the "bench"), dough—whether it is sticky and tacky or dry and hard—effortlessly comes off. It's the quickest and easiest way to clean a surface (you never want to use water when cleaning a floury surface because you'll just make paste). It's also handy for dividing bread dough into smaller pieces. It is very inexpensive and can be found in most kitchenware stores.

DIGITAL SCALE

Americans like their measuring cups and spoons, but for baking, the efficiency, speed, and accuracy of measuring by digital scale are unmatched. Everyone has a different way of measuring—if you dip and sweep a cupful of flour versus using a spoon to scoop flour and transfer it to a measuring cup, you will get a different weight measurement. Additionally, some people sift the flour first with a fork prior to scooping, which aerates the flour and also provides for a different volume measurement. Since accuracy is the key to consistent results in baking, always measure your ingredients using a digital scale. Don't skimp and buy a cheap scale, either—invest in a good-quality one that offers consistency even in small amounts. The accuracy of your scale is important.

DOUGH SCRAPER

This is the best inexpensive investment you'll ever make. This little piece of flexible plastic has a curved edge that makes removing even the stickiest mass of dough from a bowl incredibly clean and effortless. You can find dough scrapers at most kitchenware stores.

FELT-TIP PERMANENT MARKER AND MASKING TAPE

A permanent marker and a strip of masking tape are useful for labeling bowls of dough with the time at which mixing stopped. You can also mark how many folds the dough has in it if it needs to be refrigerated during the rolling and folding process (as you do with babka dough). If you plan on freezing baked or unbaked shaped bread, always mark the date on the wrapping with a marker; you want to use frozen dough— whether baked or unbaked—within 1 month.

FOOD PROCESSOR

Generally a great investment for pureeing food, shredding cheese, and making bread crumbs. Buy a food processor with a small bowl insert for small quantities of ingredients.

KITCHEN TOWELS

You can never have enough clean kitchen towels! They are great to drape over rising dough, to clear off a surface, or, when triple-folded, to pull a hot pan from the oven. Be sure to buy towels that won't leave little fuzzy bits of material behind on your dough. Linen or tightly woven cotton towels (often called tea towels) are best.

KUGELHOPF PAN

This narrow, fluted cake pan has a tube in the center; it is similar to a Bundt pan but with a smaller capacity (7 to 10 cups is typical). It is taller and narrower than a Bundt, which usually has a 12- to 15-cup capacity.

LARGE BINS AND CONTAINERS

For trouble-free measuring, transfer flour and sugar to large containers with airtight lids. Keep a scoop right in the container for easy scooping.

LARGE UNSCENTED CLEAR PLASTIC GARBAGE BAGS

You can use unscented garbage bags as homemade proof boxes for dough (see page 97). The plastic creates a humid environment where the dough can rest.

LOAF PANS

A standard-size loaf pan is 8½ by 4½ inches. If you are using higher-end stoneware rather than a metal or glass pan, be sure to measure your pan—it will likely have a different measurement, and you may need to adjust the size that you roll your dough to or change the shape of the loaf to accommodate your pan. If you are using Advanced Babka Dough (page 54) to make the babkas, you will need to buy paper loaf pans that measure 9 by 2¾ by 2 inches (visit bakedeco.com).

METAL SPATULAS

For flipping, turning, and transferring.

MIXING BOWLS

Nonreactive metal bowls in all sizes are the most practical.

PARCHMENT PAPER

Parchment paper is endlessly handy for lining baking sheets or holding sifted flour. Pick up the edges and slide the flour right into your bowl—no mess!

PASTRY BRUSH

To egg-wash dough, use natural-bristle brushes. But sometimes they get stiff and can tear the dough, so it's a good practice to let the bristles warm up under warm water to soften a bit before applying the egg wash.

RIMMED SHEET PANS

Buy three or four half-sheet pans that measure 13 by 18 inches. A couple of quarter-sheet pans (8¾ by 12¾ inches) will come in handy too.

ROLLING PIN

Forget fancy handles and decorations. All you need is a well-balanced 2- to 3-inch-diameter wooden dowel that is sanded very smooth. A French pin with tapered ends is also a great tool for rolling dough. A solid piece of wood, tapered or not, is preferable to a rolling pin with handles because you can use a rolling pin to soften butter or dough by smacking it with the pin—try doing that with a pin that has handles and see how quickly you break off the handle!

RUBBER SPATULAS

You need this tool for scraping the mixer bowl, folding the dough, and getting all the add-ins out of a measuring cup.

RULER

An old-school ruler is essential for measuring dough after rolling it out. A long ruler or yardstick (3 feet long) comes in handy, but even a standard 12-inch ruler is fine. Plastic rulers work well; the numbers on some metal rulers can wear off with time.

SAUCEPANS

Small, medium, and large saucepans—get ones with tight-fitting lids and heavy bottoms that conduct heat evenly.

SIEVE

A tamis sieve is a wide, drum-style sieve with a flat bottom (as opposed to a rounded sieve). It's the quickest and easiest way to sift flour to aerate it. However, if you don't have the storage space for a tamis, a rounded fine-mesh sieve with a handle is fine.

SKILLETS

Twelve- to 14-inch skillets are key for making Mofleta (page 34). Traditional stainless steel is better than nonstick because you can heat it at a very high temperature without worrying about ruining the pan (or releasing harmful chemicals into your food or the environment).

STAND MIXER

All you need to make bread and other baked goods are your hands . . . but a stand mixer makes the job a lot easier! A large-capacity stand mixer, one with a 5- to 7-quart bowl, generally works best for dough. You'll want to use a heavy-duty or professional mixer too. When handling the dough, you need a mixer with the most power. So while the power difference is noticeable between the small and large mixers, the price difference is negligible. A smaller-capacity bowl is okay—you just may have to stop the mixer occasionally to scrape the dough off the hook.

WIRE COOLING RACKS

Invest in at least two so you can cool multiple loaves and batches of sweets at a time.

WORK SURFACE

Use a marble board or a wooden board for kneading bread. For making ropes of challah or babka dough, a nice long work surface is helpful. If you don't have a freestanding island or lots of counter space, do what your grandmother did and use your kitchen table!

SAVORY

Challah

Makes 3 loaves (1.75 kilos/3½ pounds of dough)

Why make one challah when you can make three? Challah freezes beautifully (see the box on page 78)—you can freeze a loaf whole, or slice it and then freeze it for toast or French toast. Or have one loaf for dinner or breakfast, and give the other loaf to a friend or someone close to your heart. The offer of fresh-baked bread is a beautiful gesture that is better than any bottle of wine or store-bought hostess gift.

DOUGH

400 grams (1⅔ cups) cool-room-temperature water, plus up to another 2 tablespoons if needed

40 grams (3 tablespoons plus 2 teaspoons) fresh yeast or 15 grams (1 tablespoon plus 1¾ teaspoons) active dry yeast

1 kilo (7 cups) all-purpose flour (sifted, 11.7%), plus extra as needed and for shaping

2 large eggs

100 grams (½ cup) granulated sugar

15 grams (1 tablespoon) fine salt

75 grams (5 tablespoons) sunflower oil or canola oil or unsalted butter (at room temperature)

EGG WASH AND TOPPING

1 large egg

1 tablespoon water

Pinch of fine salt

90 grams (⅔ cup) nigella, poppy, or sesame seeds (or a combination)

---

1. Make the dough: Pour the water into the bowl of a stand mixer fitted with the dough hook. Crumble the yeast into the water and use your fingers to rub and dissolve it; if using active dry yeast, whisk the yeast into the water. Add the flour, eggs, sugar, salt, and oil.

2. Mix the dough on low speed to combine the ingredients, stopping the mixer if the dough climbs up the hook or if you need to work in dry ingredients that have settled on the bottom of the bowl. Scrape the bottom and sides of the bowl as needed. It should take about 2 minutes for the dough to come together.

continued

If there are lots of dry bits in the bottom of the bowl that just aren't getting worked in, add a tablespoon or two of water. On the other hand, if the dough looks too wet or soft, add a few pinches of flour.

> **NOTE:** Eventually, you'll be able to feel the dough and know if you need to add water or flour; it's always better to adjust the ratios when the dough is first coming together at the beginning of mixing rather than wait until the end of the kneading process, since it takes longer for ingredient additions to get worked into the dough mass at this later point and you risk overworking the dough.

3. Increase the speed to medium and knead until a smooth dough forms, about 4 minutes. You want the dough to be a bit firm.

4. Stretch and fold the dough: Lightly dust your work surface with a little flour and use a plastic dough scraper to transfer the dough from the mixing bowl to the floured surface. Use your palms to push and tear the top of the dough away from you in one stroke, then fold that section onto the middle of the dough. Give the dough a quarter turn and repeat the push/tear/fold process for about 1 minute. Then push and pull the dough against the work surface to round it into a ball.

5. Let the dough rise: Lightly dust a bowl with flour, add the dough, sprinkle just a little flour on top of the dough, and cover the bowl with plastic wrap. Set the bowl aside at room temperature until the dough has risen by about 70%, about 40 minutes (this will depend on how warm your room is—when the dough proofs in a warmer room, it will take less time than in a cooler room).

6. Divide the dough: Use the dough scraper to gently lift the dough out of the bowl and transfer it to a lightly floured work surface (take care not to press out the trapped gas in the dough). Gently pull the dough into a rectangular shape. Use a bench scraper or a chef's knife to divide the dough into 3 equal horizontal strips (you can use a kitchen scale to weigh each piece if you want to be exact). Then divide each piece into 3 smaller equal parts crosswise so you end up with a total of 9 pieces.

> **NOTE:** It is best not to have an overly floured work surface when rolling dough into cylinders, since the flour makes it hard for the dough to gain enough traction to be shaped into a rope.

7. Shape the dough: Set a piece of dough lengthwise on your work surface. Use the palm of your hand to flatten the dough into a flat rectangle; then fold the top portion over and use your palm to press the edge into the flat part of the dough. Fold and press 3 more times—the dough will end up as a cylinder about 7 inches long. Set this piece aside and repeat with the other 8 pieces.

8. Return to the first piece of dough and use both hands to roll the cylinder back and forth to form a long rope, pressing down lightly when you get to the ends of the rope so they are flattened. The rope should be about 14 inches long with tapered ends. Repeat with the remaining 8 cylinders. Lightly flour the long ropes (this allows for the strands of the braid to stay somewhat separate during baking; otherwise, they'd fuse together).

9. Pinch the ends of 3 ropes together at the top (you can place a weight on top of the ends to hold them in place) and lightly flour the dough. Braid the dough, lifting each piece up and over so the braid is more stacked than it is long; you also want it to be fatter and taller in the middle and more tapered at the ends. When you get to the end of the ropes and there is nothing left to braid, use your palm to press and seal the ends together. Repeat with the remaining 6 ropes, creating 3 braided challahs. Place the challahs on 2 parchment paper–lined rimmed sheet pans, cover them with a kitchen towel (or place them inside an unscented plastic bag; see page 97), and set them aside in a warm, draft-free spot to rise until the loaves have doubled in volume, about 40 minutes (depending on how warm the room is).

10. Adjust the oven racks to the upper-middle and lower-middle positions and preheat the oven to 425°F.

11. Test the dough: Once the challah loaves have roughly doubled in size, do the press test: Press your finger lightly into the dough, remove it, and see if the depression fills in by half. If the depression fills back in quickly and completely, the dough needs more time to rise; if you press the dough and it slightly deflates, the dough has overproofed and will be heavier and less airy after baking.

12. Bake the loaves: Make the egg wash by mixing the egg, water, and salt together in a small bowl. Gently brush the entire surface of the loaves with egg wash, taking care not to let it pool in the creases of the braids. You want a nice thin coating. Generously sprinkle the loaves with the seeds.

> **NOTE:** Try dipping the egg-washed dough facedown into a large tray of seeds and then rolling it from side to side to heavily coat the bread. If you just sprinkle a few pinches over the top, it won't look very generous or appealing after the bread has expanded and baked, so be generous with the seeds whether sprinkling or rolling.

13. Bake for 15 minutes. Rotate the bottom sheet pan to the top and the top sheet pan to the bottom (turning each sheet around as you go) and bake until the loaves are golden brown, about 10 minutes longer. Remove the loaves from the oven and set them aside to cool completely on the sheet pans.

continued

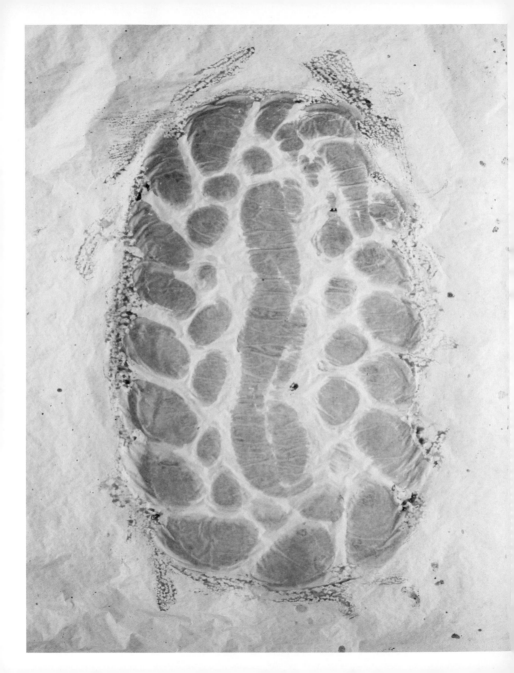

THREE IMPORTANT TIPS FOR CHALLAH

When you break into a loaf of challah, it should pull apart like cotton candy coming off the paper cone. It is layered with sheets of tender gluten, so it can be almost unraveled rather than broken apart like a loaf of sandwich bread. There are three ways to achieve this:

1. Underknead. Slightly underknead the dough so it is not worked to the gluten's full potential. With most dough, you want to be able to stretch a small corner to a thin sheet without it tearing (this is called the windowpane test). With challah, you don't want the gluten to get that strong—so knead it only as instructed.

2. Underproof. Slightly underproof the challah, meaning that when you press a finger into the rising dough, the depression that's left fills in about halfway. If the depression remains after you remove your finger, the challah is overproofed.

3. Use high heat to seal in moisture. Bake the challah in a hot oven to get the crust to form fast. A nice crust seals in moisture so the interior crumb is delicate and supple and doesn't dry out. You don't want challah to have a hearty, crisp crust—you just want the crust to be substantial enough to lock in moisture during baking but soft enough to easily rip by hand when eating.

THE SYMBOLISM OF CHALLAH

There is a lot of folklore and symbolism behind challah, especially in the braiding. Some people say the braids represent unity and love because they look like arms intertwining. Three-strand braids symbolize truth, peace, and justice; round loaves that have no beginning or end symbolize continuity or a complete year (which is why many people bake round loaves for Rosh Hashanah, the Jewish New Year). But mainly, braiding challah marks it as special enough for the Shabbat table. There are many ways to make your challah stand out. Turn to pages 24 and 26 for ideas and inspiration.

Black Tie Challah

Makes 1 loaf (580 grams/1 pound 4 ounces of dough)

This challah has a thin raised braid running lengthwise on top of the braided dough. To make it even more striking, coat the thin braid in nigella seeds (black sesame seeds work too), then coat the sides of the challah loaf in white sesame seeds so the starkness of the black nigella braid stands out.

1. After dividing the challah dough into three 550-gram (1 pound 1 ounce) pieces as described in step 6 on page 20, take about 50 grams (1¾ ounces) from 1 piece of dough and set it aside. Divide the resulting 500-gram (17-ounce) piece of dough into 3 smaller pieces and flatten, fold, and roll each piece into a rope with tapered edges, as described in steps 7 and 8 on pages 20 and 21. Repeat this process with the 50-gram (1¾-ounce) piece of dough, dividing it into thirds, flattening, folding, and pressing each piece into a cylinder and then rolling them into thin ropes about 12 inches in length. Set all the pieces aside, covered, to rest for a few minutes. Then stretch each of these thin ropes until it is about 20 inches long, lightly flour each piece, and braid them. Follow the instructions on page 21 to braid the 3 larger ropes of dough into a challah loaf.

2. Make the egg wash (see Note on page 26) and set it aside. On a piece of parchment paper, spread about 1 cup of nigella seeds in a long, thin strip. Brush the skinny braid with egg wash, then dip the braid, sticky-side down, in the nigella seeds to evenly coat it. Brush the larger braid with egg wash, then set the long nigella-coated braid right down the middle of the larger loaf. You can pinch the ends together and then tuck them under, or just gently press them onto the end of the loaf and leave them somewhat loose (the "loose ends" fan out as they bake). Generously coat the sides of the large challah with white sesame seeds. Follow the rising instructions in step 9 on page 21, then bake.

continued

Crazy and Festive Challah

Making bread doesn't have to be serious or scary. Leave the ends of the challah loose like fingers on a hand (like the hamsa, a famous good-luck symbol), or overlay other twists of challah on top of the dough to create an almost Medusa-like shape that is at once otherworldly and completely organic. Play with the dough. Leave the ends open, or twist instead of braid. Try different seeds—pumpkin seeds, nigella seeds, black sesame seeds, sunflower seeds. Bake a bowl into the bread (an oven-safe bowl, of course), or bake three bowls into it!

While you're shaping the bread, remember not to weave the strands or shapes too tightly—make sure you leave enough room for the dough to expand during the proofing stage. Also remember to flour all the individual pieces before braiding so the strands remain separate during baking. A fine dusting is all it takes. This really helps the final shape stand out.

> **NOTE:** When egg-washing the challah, do so with a light hand—no one wants a pocket of scrambled egg in their challah braid! Apply the egg wash from one direction and then turn the sheet pan around to brush in the other direction as well, so you're sure to evenly coat all of the surfaces. A spray bottle works well too—it applies an even spritz without the risk of tearing or marring the dough.

Whole Wheat and Flax Challah

Makes 3 loaves (1.5 kilos/3⅓ pounds of dough)

For this challah, some whole wheat flour is incorporated with the white flour, along with red quinoa, flaxseeds, and molasses-y brown sugar instead of white. Because the seeds and flour are moisture-hungry, there is 5 to 10% more water in this recipe than in others. Keep a little extra water next to the mixer bowl in case your dough needs it (it will depend on the kind of whole wheat flour you are using).

The coil shape of this challah is common during Rosh Hashanah, symbolizing the completeness and continuity of the year that has passed and the one that lies ahead. As with all the challahs in this chapter, you can shape the dough any way you'd like.

100 grams (½ cup plus 2 tablespoons) whole flaxseeds

100 grams (⅔ cup) red quinoa

240 grams (1 cup) steaming-hot water

180 grams (¾ cup) ice-cold water

35 grams (¼ cup) fresh yeast or 10 grams (2 teaspoons) active dry yeast

400 grams (3½ cups) whole wheat flour (sifted)

320 grams (2½ cups) all-purpose flour (sifted, 11.7%), plus extra as needed and for shaping

2 large eggs

50 grams (¼ cup, packed, plus 1 tablespoon) dark brown sugar

15 grams (1 tablespoon) fine salt

60 grams (¼ cup) sunflower oil or canola oil or unsalted butter (at room temperature)

EGG WASH AND TOPPING

1 large egg

1 tablespoon water

Pinch of fine salt

50 grams (¼ cup) millet seeds

1. Soak the flaxseeds and quinoa: Place the flaxseeds and quinoa in a large heat-safe bowl or container and cover with the hot water. Stir, cover the bowl, and set aside for at least 30 minutes, or up to overnight, to soften.

2. Make the dough: Fill a small bowl with ice and water and stir for a few seconds to allow the water to get icy cold. Measure out ¾ cup of the ice-cold water and pour it into the bowl of a stand mixer fitted with the dough hook. Crumble the yeast into the water and use your fingers to rub and dissolve it; if using active dry yeast, whisk the yeast into the water. Add the whole wheat flour, all-purpose flour, flaxseed mixture, eggs, brown sugar, salt, and oil.

> **NOTE:** If you want to use whole wheat flour in combination with white flour in a recipe, you will probably have to increase the liquid in the recipe by 5 to 10% because the whole wheat flour absorbs more water. The same is true for adding seeds: When adding seeds like flax or millet to a recipe, you will need to presoak them and increase the amount of liquid in the recipe since they will absorb a lot of liquid on their own.

3. Mix the dough on low speed to combine the ingredients, stopping the mixer if the dough climbs up the hook or if you need to work in dry ingredients that have settled on the bottom of the bowl. Scrape the bottom and sides of the bowl as needed. It should take about 2 minutes for the dough to come together.

4. Increase the speed to medium and knead until a smooth dough forms, about 4 minutes. You may need to add a little water if the dough is too stiff, or a little flour if it is too slack.

5. Stretch and fold the dough: Lightly dust your work surface with a little flour and use a plastic dough scraper to transfer the dough from the mixing bowl to the floured surface. Use your palms to push and tear the top of the dough away from you in one stroke, then fold that section onto the middle of the dough. Give the dough a quarter turn and repeat the push/tear/fold process for about 1 minute. Then push and pull the dough against the work surface to round it into a ball.

6. Let the dough rise: Lightly dust a bowl with flour, add the dough, sprinkle just a little flour on top of the dough, and cover the bowl with plastic wrap. Set the bowl aside at room temperature until the dough has risen by about 70%, about 40 minutes (this will depend on how warm your room is —when the dough proofs in a warmer room, it will take less time than in a cooler room).

7. Divide the dough: Gently use the dough scraper to help lift the dough out of the bowl and onto a lightly floured work surface (take care not to press out the trapped gas in the dough) and divide the dough into 3 equal parts (you can use a kitchen scale to weigh each piece if you want to be exact).

8. Shape the dough: Set the dough lengthwise on your work surface and use the palm of your hand to flatten 1 piece of the dough into a flat rectangle; then fold the top portion over and use your palm to press the edge into the flat part of the dough. Fold and press 3 more times—

the dough will end up as a long cylinder, about 30 inches long and 2 inches thick. Repeat with the other pieces of dough.

9. Return to the first piece of dough and use both hands to roll the cylinder back and forth to form a long rope, 4 to 4½ feet (48 to 54 inches) long, lifting one end in each hand and slapping the center of the rope against the table to elongate it if it gets tight and resists rolling. Repeat with the other 2 pieces of dough. Lightly flour the long ropes (this allows for the coils in the spiral to stay somewhat separate during baking; otherwise, they'd fuse together).

10. Line 2 rimmed sheet pans with parchment paper (you will probably bake 2 loaves on 1 prepared sheet pan and 1 loaf on the other). Wind 1 rope into a spiral on one of the prepared sheet pans, tucking the end up through the middle to make a little button. Repeat with the other 2 ropes on the second prepared sheet pan. Cover each sheet pan with a kitchen towel (or set inside an unscented plastic bag; see page 97) and set it aside in a warm, draft-free spot to rise until the spirals have doubled in volume, about 1 hour (depending on how warm the room is).

11. Adjust the oven racks to the upper-middle and lower-middle positions and preheat the oven to 350°F.

12. Test the dough: Once the dough has roughly doubled in size, do the press test: Press your finger lightly into the dough, remove it, and see if the depression fills in by half. If the depression fills back in, the dough needs more time to rise.

13. Bake the loaves: Make the egg wash by mixing the egg, water, and salt together in a small bowl. Gently brush the entire surface of the loaves with egg wash, taking care not to let it pool in the creases of the spirals. You want a nice thin coating. Sprinkle the top of each spiral with millet seeds.

> **NOTE:** Baking this loaf with a little steam will create an airy crumb. When preheating your oven, place a rimmed sheet pan on the floor of the oven (or if that is not possible, on the lowest oven rack). When you place the bread in the oven, add about ¼ cup water to the sheet pan and quickly close the oven door. The water hitting the hot pan will create steam.

14. Bake the challah for 15 minutes. Then rotate the bottom challah to the top and the top challah to the bottom (turning the baking sheets too) and continue to bake until the loaves are golden brown, about 10 minutes longer. Remove the loaves from the oven and set them aside to cool.

Jachnun

Makes 10 pieces

Jachnun, a heavy, crêpe-like Yemenite bread, is most often served with grated tomato and spicy *z'hug* (a Yemenite hot sauce) on Saturdays as part of the Sabbath brunch. Observant Jews who don't cook on Saturdays place a tightly covered pan of jachnun in a barely warm oven on Friday night (or drop the tin in the embers of a *taboon*) and slow-bake it until they pull it out on Saturday and serve it for lunch. Traditionally one egg for each guest is baked on top of the dough within the sealed tin; when the eggs are peeled and quartered the next day, the shell and the white are deeply browned. The egg makes the meal complete, while the grated tomato and *z'hug* add a light, fresh, peppery counterpoint.

1 kilo (8 cups) all-purpose flour (sifted, 11.7%)

50 grams (¼ cup) granulated sugar

2 grams (½ teaspoon) baking powder

35 grams (2 tablespoons) honey

20 grams (1 tablespoon plus 1 teaspoon) fine salt

675 grams (2½ cups plus 1 tablespoon) warm water

15 grams (1 tablespoon) vegetable oil

200 grams (1 stick plus 5 tablespoons) unsalted butter (very soft—nearly melted)

10 large eggs

2 large ripe tomatoes, grated on the large-hole side of a box grater

Red or green z'hug

1. Make the dough: Place the flour, sugar, baking powder, honey, and salt in a large bowl. Add the water to the bowl and stir until the dough is shaggy and the water has been absorbed. Knead the dough in the bowl for 2 minutes (it will be pretty wet and sticky). Set the dough aside at room temperature to rest for 5 minutes.

2. Knead the dough: Slide your hand beneath the dough toward the center so your fingers point up (beneath the dough). Lift the dough from the middle, moving your hand toward the edge of the bowl to stretch it. Release the dough, give the bowl a quarter turn, and repeat 7 times. Cover the bowl with plastic wrap and set the dough aside to rest at room temperature for 1 hour.

continued

3. Divide the dough and shape it:
Lightly oil a large plate. Oil your hand and pat some oil under the dough and over the surface. Grab a corner of the dough and squeeze your forefinger and thumb around it, pushing a baseball-size ball of dough up through the circle made by your finger and thumb. Break off the ball, place your thumb in the center of the ball, and use your other hand to fold the edges over your thumb, using your thumb to pinch down each of the edges as they get folded over. Pinch all the corners shut and then set the dough on the oiled plate, smooth-side up. Repeat with the remaining pieces of dough to make 10 baseball-size balls. Cover the dough loosely with a kitchen towel and let it rest at room temperature for 5 minutes.

4. Adjust an oven rack to the lowest position and preheat the oven to 225°F.

5. Stretch and shape the dough: Fold a long piece of parchment paper in half lengthwise and place it across the bottom of an 8-inch springform pan or kubaneh pan (see page 37) so the edges of the parchment hang over the sides (like a sling). Heavily butter your work surface and set a ball of dough on top. Butter the top of the dough and use your hands to push and stretch the dough into a paper-thin rectangle (stretch it as far as you can without the dough tearing, adding more butter as needed to prevent tearing—but don't worry if it tears). Fold the left side of the rectangle over the center, lightly butter the top of the fold, then fold the right side over (creating a simple fold; see the box on page 55) and lightly butter the top. Starting at a narrow edge, roll the dough into a tight cylinder. Set the cylinder in the prepared pan, perpendicular to the length of the paper. Repeat with 3 more balls. Once the first layer of the pan is full, set the next layer on top of the first, across the first layer in a crosshatch pattern. Place the final 2 cylinders around the edges of the pan.

6. Bake the jachnun: Butter another doubled sheet of parchment paper and place it, buttered-side down, on top of the dough. Place the (unpeeled) eggs on top of the parchment, then cover the pan with aluminum foil, crimping it around the edges to seal the pan (if you're using a kubaneh pan, you can skip that step and just put the lid in place). Place the pan in the oven and set a sheet pan on top of the foil (unless there is a kubaneh lid). Bake the jachnun overnight, for 12 hours.

7. The next morning, remove the jachnun from the oven. Uncover the pan, set the eggs aside, and discard the parchment paper. Place the jachnun on a platter. Peel the eggs and arrange them around the jachnun. Serve with the grated tomato and z'hug alongside.

Mofleta

Makes one 14-inch pan of mofleta (about 24 sheets)

In Morocco, at the end of Pesach, a sweet feast called Mimouna celebrates the return of the leavened foods and wheat that are forbidden during the eight days of Passover. In the earliest days of the tradition, at the end of the holiday, family, friends, and Muslim neighbors were invited to Jewish homes to enjoy cakes and cookies and pastries. Now this tradition is celebrated throughout Israel, too, and it is an excuse to have a wonderful dessert party! One of the classic dishes served is mofleta, a stack of thin yeasted crêpes that are smeared with butter, drizzled with honey, rolled like a cigar, and then eaten by hand.

300 grams (1 cup plus 3 tablespoons) cool-room-temperature water

15 grams (2 tablespoons) fresh yeast or 5 grams (1 teaspoon) active dry yeast

500 grams (4¾ cups) cake flour or white pastry flour (sifted, 8 to 9%), plus extra for kneading and shaping

5 grams (1 teaspoon) granulated sugar

½ teaspoon fine salt

720 to 960 grams (3 to 4 cups) neutral oil

Unsalted butter (at room temperature), for serving

Honey, for serving

1. Make the dough: Pour the water into the bowl of a stand mixer fitted with the dough hook. Crumble the yeast into the water and use your fingers to rub and dissolve it; if using active dry yeast, whisk the yeast into the water. Add the flour, sugar, and salt and mix on low speed until the dough comes together into a semismooth ball, about 2 minutes.

2. Stretch and fold the dough: Transfer the dough to a lightly floured work surface. Stretch one corner of the dough out and fold it on top of the middle of the dough. Give the dough a quarter turn and repeat a few more times, until each corner has been stretched and folded twice to make a nicely shaped ball.

3. Let the dough rise: Lightly flour a large bowl and set the dough in the bowl; sprinkle the top with a little flour, cover the bowl with plastic wrap, and set aside at room temperature until nearly doubled in volume, about 30 minutes.

continued

4. Divide the dough and shape into balls: Pour 3 cups of the oil into a large bowl and set it aside. Lightly flour your work surface and set the dough on top. Pat and stretch the dough into an 8-by-12-inch rectangle that is as even as possible. Use a bench scraper to divide the dough lengthwise into 4 equal strips and then into 6 strips crosswise, to yield 24 pieces. Holding a piece of dough in your hand, stretch one-quarter of the piece up and over onto the middle. Repeat with the other 3 sides to create a rough ball shape. Place the dough, seam-side down, on the work surface and repeat with the remaining pieces.

5. Wipe the excess flour from the work surface and cup your hand around a piece of dough. Push and pull the dough in a circular motion on the work surface until it is rounded into a tight ball with hardly a seam at the bottom and drop the dough ball into the bowl of oil. Repeat with the other pieces of dough. Once all the dough has been shaped, let the balls rest in the oil for 10 minutes (add more oil as needed to make sure the balls are completely covered; you don't want them to dry out).

6. Stretch and cook the dough: Set a dough ball on the work surface. Using your hands, stretch and push it into a paper-thin sheet (try not to create holes, but if you get a few, it's okay). It should stretch very easily. Heat a large nonstick skillet over medium-high heat. Reduce the heat to medium and carefully lay the sheet in the pan. While the first piece of dough cooks, stretch another piece. Once the dough in the skillet starts to become golden brown, after about 2 minutes, use a spatula to carefully flip it over. Lay the second sheet of stretched dough on top of the first in the skillet. Stretch your next piece of dough. When the underside of the dough in the pan is golden brown, after another 2 to 3 minutes (adjust the heat as needed so the dough doesn't get too dark), carefully flip the 2 layers over together and place the just-stretched piece on top of the stack. Repeat this process, stretching, flipping, and adding to the dough stack, until all the dough pieces are stacked in the skillet like a giant flatbread layer cake. Remove the stack from the skillet and place it on a large plate.

7. Serve the mofleta with lots of butter and honey. To eat, peel away a layer of mofleta, add a smear of butter and a drizzle of honey, and roll it into a cylinder. Mofleta is best eaten while hot.

Kubaneh

Makes one 9-inch round loaf (860 grams/1 pound 14 ounces of dough)

Kubaneh, a rich Yemenite bread, is a cross between a brioche and a flatbread. The bread is traditionally started on Friday, when the dough is prepared and shaped; the pieces of dough are stacked in a special lidded tin and baked overnight (similar to jachnun, another Yemenite flatbread made without yeast; see page 31). The tin is pulled from the oven on Saturday and served for lunch with grated tomato and z'hug (a Yemenite hot sauce).

Classic kubaneh is baked in a covered pan that holds in all the steam. This version doesn't require you to bake the kubanch overnight (see page 40); instead, it is baked in a moderately warm oven, making the cover unnecessary. As the bread grows and expands, you can see all the layers created during the shaping.

290 grams (1¼ cups) cool-room-temperature water

20 grams (2½ tablespoons) fresh yeast or 8 grams (2¼ teaspoons) active dry yeast

500 grams (4 cups) all-purpose flour (sifted, 11.7%), plus extra for shaping

60 grams (¼ cup) granulated sugar

20 grams (1 tablespoon plus 1 teaspoon) fine salt

150 grams (1¼ sticks) unsalted butter, cut into small pieces

2 ripe tomatoes, grated on the large-hole side of a box grater

1. Make the dough: Pour the water into the bowl of a stand mixer fitted with the dough hook. Crumble the yeast into the water and use your fingers to rub and dissolve it; if using active dry yeast, whisk the yeast into the water. Add the flour, sugar, and salt.

2. Mix the dough on low speed to combine the ingredients, stopping the mixer if the dough climbs up the hook or if you need to work in dry ingredients

that have settled on the bottom of the bowl. Scrape the bottom and sides of the bowl as needed. Once the dough comes together, increase the speed to medium-high and continue to knead until the dough cleans the bottom and sides of the bowl, about 3 minutes.

3. Stretch and fold the dough: Lightly dust your work surface with a little flour and use a plastic dough scraper to transfer the dough from the mixing bowl to the

floured surface. Use your palms to stretch a corner of the dough away from you in one stroke, then fold the front portion over and on top of itself. Give the dough a quarter turn and repeat. Do this about 10 times, until the dough is shaped into a nice smooth round.

4. Let the dough rise: Lightly flour a large bowl, set the dough in the bowl, lightly flour the top of the dough, and cover the bowl with plastic wrap. Set the bowl aside at room temperature until the dough has almost doubled in volume, about 30 minutes (depending on the warmth of the room).

5. Divide and shape the dough: Place the butter in a microwave-safe dish and heat it in the microwave just until it is very soft and perhaps 25% melted, 10 seconds or so. Lightly grease a large plate with a little bit of the butter. Lightly flour your work surface and set the dough on top. Divide it into 8 equal pieces. Cup your hand around a piece of dough and then push and pull it, rolling it against the work surface, to gently shape it into a ball. Set the ball on the buttered plate and repeat with the remaining pieces of dough. Cover the plate with plastic wrap and set it aside at room temperature for 30 minutes.

6. Stretch the dough: Use about 2 tablespoons of the softened butter to generously grease a 9-inch springform pan, or use a smaller springform pan or

a kubaneh pan. Take about a tablespoon of the butter and use it to grease your clean, nonfloured work surface. Take a ball of dough from the plate, smear another tablespoon of butter on top of it, and gently press and spread it out to form a paper-thin 12- to 13-inch square. Use more butter as needed—you want to use a lot! The butter helps spread the dough very thin without tearing (but don't worry if it tears).

7. Shape the dough: Fold the left side of the dough over the center, then the right side over the left to create a simple fold (see the box on page 55). Starting at the bottom of the strip, roll the dough into a tight cylinder. Slice the cylinder in half crosswise, then place the halves in the prepared springform pan, with the cut side facing up. Repeat with the remaining balls of dough (reserve 1 tablespoon of butter to use in step 10), arranging the pieces in a circle in the pan with a few pieces in the center. If you're using a smaller springform or a kubaneh pan, stack the dough (as you would for monkey bread). If you're using a springform pan, wrap the bottom of the pan in a large sheet of aluminum foil just in case any butter drips out (this will prevent the butter from burning and smoking up the oven). If you're using a kubaneh pan, you can skip this step.

8. Let the kubaneh proof: Cover the pan with plastic wrap and set it aside in a warm, draft-free place until a finger gently pressed into the dough leaves a depression that quickly fills in by three-quarters, about 40 minutes (depending on how warm the room is).

9. Preheat the oven to 350°F.

10. Bake the kubaneh: Melt the reserved 1 tablespoon butter, brush it over the top of the dough, and place the pan in the oven. After 15 minutes, reduce the oven temperature to 325°F and bake until the top is deeply golden, 30 to 40 minutes. Remove the pan from the oven and set it aside to cool for at least 20 minutes before turning the bread out of the pan.

11. To serve, invert the bread onto a platter so the pretty side faces up. Let people rip the kubaneh apart, separating the bread into small rolls. Serve the grated tomato on the side.

Variation

Traditional "Overnight" Kubaneh

Follow the Kubaneh recipe through step 8. Preheat the oven to 225°F. Set a sheet of aluminum foil on your work surface and smear some of the butter in the center of the foil to make a 9-inch round. Remove the plastic wrap from the pan and invert the aluminum foil over the pan so the buttered area is centered over the dough; then tightly crimp the foil around the top of the pan.

Place the pan in the oven and set a heavy baking sheet on top of it to ensure that no steam escapes (if using a kubaneh pan, just place the lid on the pan). Bake for 4½ hours. Turn off the oven and leave the bread in the oven until you're ready to serve it.

To serve, remove the foil (or kubaneh pan lid) and turn out the bread; then invert it onto a platter so the pretty side faces up. Let people rip the kubaneh apart, separating the clusters into small rolls.

Savory Potato Hamantaschen

Makes 24 to 30 hamantaschen

Hamantaschen are triangular shortbread cookies traditionally filled with poppy seeds or apricot or other sweets; they are made for Purim (a Jewish holiday with elements of Halloween). This version uses pie dough stuffed with a savory filling to make something that is close to a turnover like a bureka. Savory hamantaschen are excellent as little appetizers to serve at a cocktail party. The dough does need to rest for some time—ideally overnight—so plan ahead. **Pictured on page 45**

PIE DOUGH

350 grams (1¾ cups) all-purpose flour (sifted, 11.7%), plus extra for dusting and shaping

250 grams (2 sticks) unsalted butter (freezer chilled, not frozen)

70 grams (¼ cup plus 2 teaspoons) ice water, plus up to another 2 teaspoons if needed

5 grams (¾ teaspoon) granulated sugar

5 grams (1 teaspoon) fine salt

POTATO FILLING

2 Yukon gold potatoes, peeled and cut into ½-inch cubes

20 grams (4 teaspoons) fine salt, plus a pinch

15 grams (about 3 tablespoons) fresh flat-leaf parsley leaves, roughly chopped

5 grams (1 teaspoon) extra-virgin olive oil

20 grams (scant 1½ tablespoons) mayonnaise

EGG WASH AND TOPPING

1 large egg

1 tablespoon water

Pinch of kosher salt

75 grams (½ cup) black sesame seeds

1. Make the pie dough: Place the flour in the bowl of a stand mixer and chill it in the freezer for 20 minutes. Remove the bowl from the freezer and set it on your work surface. Sprinkle a little of the flour over the butter and, working quickly so the butter doesn't warm up, cut the butter crosswise into very thin pieces. Sprinkle the pieces of butter with a little more of the cold flour and chop them very fine, until the butter looks like grated cheese. If the butter starts to warm up and soften, put it in a bowl and freeze it for 10 minutes before continuing.

2. Fill a small bowl with ice and water and stir for a few seconds to allow the water to get icy cold. Measure out ¼ cup plus 2 teaspoons of the ice water and pour it into a large bowl. Add the sugar and salt and whisk until dissolved.

3. Use a bench scraper to transfer the butter and any bits of flour from the work surface to the mixer bowl containing the remaining flour. Set the bowl onto the stand mixer, attach the paddle, and cut the butter into the flour on medium-low speed until there aren't many pieces left that are larger than a small lentil, about 2 minutes.

4. With the mixer running, pour 3 tablespoons of the water mixture over the flour mixture, adding it around the edges of the bowl. Let the mixer run for 10 seconds, then stop the mixer and grab and squeeze the dough several times

with your hands. Return the mixer to medium-low speed, add the remaining water around the edges of the bowl, and let the mixer run for a few seconds. The dough should start to come together but still be crumbly around the edges of the bowl (if it doesn't come together, add up to another 2 teaspoons of ice water). Stop the mixer and squeeze a small knob of dough in your hand. It should hold together. If it crumbles or feels dry, add a little more water, a small spoonful at a time, until the dough holds together without crumbling apart.

5. Transfer the dough (it will be crumbly) to a lightly floured work surface. Press and squeeze the dough into a mound, then knead it 3 times. Press it into a ¾-inch-thick square and wrap it in plastic wrap. Refrigerate the dough for at least 30 minutes or up to 2 days (an overnight rest in the refrigerator is best for well-chilled and well-relaxed dough).

6. Make the filling: Bring a large pot of water to a boil over high heat. Add the potatoes and 10 grams (2 teaspoons) of the salt and cook until the potatoes are just tender, 12 to 15 minutes. Drain the potatoes in a colander or fine-mesh sieve and set aside to cool completely. Place them in a large bowl and stir in the remaining 10 grams (2 teaspoons) salt, the parsley, olive oil, and mayonnaise.

7. Flour the work surface and set the dough on top; lightly dust the top of the dough with flour. Roll the dough to form a very thin square about $\frac{1}{16}$ inch thick, dusting the top of the dough with flour and dusting beneath the dough as necessary to keep it from sticking to the work surface.

8. Use a 4-inch round cookie cutter to stamp out as many rounds as possible from the sheet of dough (you should get about 24). Gather the scraps, gently press them together (don't knead the dough—just press it so it holds together), and refrigerate for 20 minutes.

9. While the dough scraps are chilling, make the egg wash: In a small bowl, whisk the egg, water, and kosher salt together. Pour the sesame seeds into a shallow dish. Brush the entire surface of each dough round with egg wash and then press the egg-washed side into the sesame seeds. Set the rounds, sesame-side down, on a parchment paper–lined rimmed sheet pan and brush them with more egg wash. Chill the rounds in the refrigerator for 20 minutes if they have become too soft to work with easily.

10. Set a small bowl of water on your work surface and use a pastry brush to lightly dab the outer edges of each

hamantaschen round. Add 1 heaping tablespoon of the potato filling to the center of each round. Use your thumb and forefinger to pinch 2 edges of the dough together, then pinch the other edges together to create the classic triangle-shaped hamantaschen (see the photo on page 45). Place the filled hamantaschen in the refrigerator for at least 20 minutes (or up to overnight) to chill before baking.

11. Flour the work surface, place the dough scrap ball on top, flour the top, and roll it into a very thin square as before. Cut out as many rounds as possible and repeat steps 9 and 10. Discard any remaining dough scraps.

12. Preheat the oven to 375°F.

13. Bake the hamantaschen until browned, 10 to 15 minutes. Remove from the oven and let them cool completely on the sheet pan before serving.

> **NOTE:** If you plan on freezing pie dough to use in a month or two, add 2 or 3 drops of distilled white vinegar to the water-sugar-salt mixture before adding it to the flour-butter mixture. The vinegar in the dough preserves it and prevents it from getting speckled dark spots.

Beet Hamantaschen

Makes 24 to 30 hamantaschen

This savory hamantaschen with its beet and hazelnut filling makes a great meal—add a plate of hummus, some olives, maybe some pita or a bureka, and you're set. In most grocery stores, it is more common to find unskinned than peeled hazelnuts. To easily remove the skin, roast the nuts at 350°F until they are fragrant and toasted, usually 6 to 8 minutes (use your timer—when nuts roast too long, they turn bitter and burnt very quickly and you'll have to start over), then rub them in a cloth while they are still warm. The skins will, for the most part, just flake away.

All-purpose flour for rolling and shaping

1 recipe hamantaschen pie dough (page 41), prepared through step 5

1 large egg

1 tablespoon water

Pinch of kosher salt

75 grams (½ cup) black sesame seeds

255 grams (9 ounces; about 2 beets) roasted beets, chopped into ½-inch pieces

30 grams (1 ounce) toasted and skinned hazelnuts, finely chopped

3 garlic cloves, minced

1 bunch fresh cilantro leaves, finely chopped (about ½ cup)

10 grams (2 teaspoons) extra-virgin olive oil

¾ teaspoon fine salt

½ teaspoon freshly ground black pepper

135 grams (heaping 1 cup) goat's- or sheep's-milk feta cheese, crumbled

1. Flour a work surface, set the dough on top, and lightly dust the top of the dough with flour. Roll the dough to form a very thin square about ¹⁄₁₆ inch thick, dusting the top of the dough with flour and dusting beneath the dough as necessary to keep it from sticking to the work surface.

2. Use a 4-inch round cookie cutter to stamp out as many rounds as possible from the sheet of dough (you should get about 24). Gather the scraps, gently press them together (don't knead the dough—just press it so it holds together), and refrigerate for 20 minutes.

continued

3. While the dough scraps are chilling, make the egg wash: In a small bowl, whisk the egg, water, and kosher salt together. Pour the sesame seeds into a shallow dish. Brush the entire surface of each dough round with egg wash and then press the egg-washed side into the sesame seeds. Set the rounds, sesame-side down, on a parchment paper–lined rimmed sheet pan and brush them with more egg wash. Chill the rounds in the refrigerator for 20 minutes if they have become too soft to work with easily.

4. Make the filling: Place the beets, hazelnuts, garlic, cilantro, olive oil, salt, and pepper in a large bowl and toss to lightly combine. Add the feta and stir once or twice (you don't want the feta to color too much from the beets).

5. Set a small bowl of water on your work surface and use a pastry brush to lightly dab the outer edges of each hamantaschen round. Add 1 heaping tablespoon of the beet filling to the center of each round. Use your thumb and forefinger to pinch 2 edges of the dough together, then pinch the other edges together to create the classic triangle-shaped hamantaschen (see the photo on page 45). Place the filled hamantaschen in the refrigerator for at least 20 minutes (or up to overnight) to chill before baking.

6. Flour the work surface, place the dough scrap ball on top, flour the top, and roll it into a very thin square as before. Cut out as many rounds as possible and repeat steps 3 and 5.

7. Preheat the oven to 375°F.

8. Bake the hamantaschen until browned, 12 to 15 minutes. Remove from the oven and let them cool completely on the sheet pan before serving.

Spinach Burekas

Makes 8 burekas

In Israel, you know the filling of the bureka according to its shape. Triangular burekas are almost always filled with cheese, and rectangular ones with potato or spinach (spinach burekas are also sometimes shaped into a coil or snail). The pastry gets crispier and flakier around all the edges if shaped in a rectangle. **Pictured on pages 16 and 17**

15 grams (1 tablespoon) extra-virgin olive oil

½ yellow onion, diced

1 large garlic clove, minced

300 grams (10½ ounces; about 10 cups) fresh spinach, tough stems removed, leaves coarsely chopped

1 large egg

120 grams (heaping 1 cup) feta cheese, crumbled

70 grams (⅓ cup) cream cheese (at room temperature)

40 grams (¼ cup plus 1 tablespoon) all-purpose flour, plus extra for rolling and shaping

Fine salt

Freshly ground black pepper

1 teaspoon water

455 grams (1 pound) store-bought puff pastry (see page 49), thawed if frozen

110 grams (⅔ cup) sesame seeds, poppy seeds, or nigella seeds (or a combination)

1. Heat the olive oil in a large skillet over medium heat. Add the onion, reduce the heat to medium-low, and cook, stirring occasionally, until it starts to brown, 7 to 8 minutes. Add the garlic and cook, stirring often, until it is fragrant, about 30 seconds; then stir in about half the spinach and cook until it starts to wilt, 2 minutes. Add the remaining spinach and cook, stirring and turning the mixture, until it is mostly wilted, 2 to 3 minutes longer. Transfer the spinach mixture to a large bowl and let it cool.

2. Whisk the egg in a medium bowl and transfer about 1 tablespoon of the beaten egg to a small bowl (this will be for your egg wash); set that aside. Mix the feta cheese and cream cheese into the remaining egg in the medium bowl, then mix in the flour until smooth. Add the cooled spinach mixture along with a few pinches of salt (be careful when adding salt since feta cheese is salty) and a couple grinds of black pepper.

continued

3. Add the water and a pinch of salt to the reserved beaten egg and whisk to combine. Set the puff pastry on a lightly floured work surface and roll it into a rectangle approximately 10 by 15 inches and about ⅛ inch thick, with a long side facing you. Divide the dough into 8 rectangles. Brush the bottom third of each rectangle with some of the egg wash (reserve the remainder of the egg wash). Spoon (or pipe) about 2 tablespoons of the spinach mixture in a line across the bottom third of the dough and then fold the top over to meet the bottom (egg-washed) edge. Do not press the edges to seal. Instead, lightly tap them together about ⅛ inch in from the edge, then use your finger to press down and seal the rectangle along this line (this is so the edges puff when baked, letting you see the layers of the pastry at the edge of the bureka).

4. Set the burekas on a parchment paper–lined sheet pan and refrigerate for at least 20 minutes and up to 24 hours (if refrigerating them longer than 1 hour, cover the sheet pan with plastic wrap).

5. Preheat the oven to 400°F.

6. Remove the burekas from the refrigerator and brush the top of each one with the remaining egg wash. Sprinkle each bureka generously with the seeds, then use a paring knife to score the top of each one 2 or 3 times. Bake the burekas until they are puffed and golden brown, about 25 minutes. Let them cool slightly before serving.

BUYING PUFF PASTRY

Making puff pastry dough is no minor task—it takes numerous hours and a lot of patience. Not many of us have the time and energy to make homemade puff pastry, but there are good-quality frozen brands for sale in higher-end grocery stores (or ask your local baker to sell some to you). Look for one made with all butter, as it will have the very best flavor. Additionally, some sheets are sold as rectangles and some as rounds. Buy the puff pastry in rectangular sheets if possible; it will be easier to divide into squares or rectangles for burekas or other pastries. Try to find the kind that comes as one pound to a box, but if the pastry weighs a few ounces less, it's really no big deal and shouldn't prevent you from making the burekas.

To defrost the pastry, let it sit in your refrigerator for a few hours. Unwrap it and work quickly, always refrigerating the dough if it starts to become very sticky. You want to keep puff pastry very cold so that when it goes into the oven to bake, the butter layers create lots and lots of flaky layers in your burekas (or whatever it is that you are making). If when you unroll the dough, it looks speckled with little black gray dots, this means it is not fresh. You should bring the dough back to the store where you bought it and get a new package (old dough isn't harmful, but puff pastry dough is not inexpensive to buy, so why settle for something that is not 100% perfect?).

SWEET

Basic Babka Dough

Makes about 900 grams (2 pounds) of dough, for two 9-by-5-inch babkas

This simple babka dough will yield a very rich and delicious babka. And if you want an even richer, flakier version, try out the Advanced Babka Dough on page 54. Making babka takes less than an hour of actual work—the rest of the time is the proofing and the baking. You can shape the cake into a twisted loaf, or bake it in smaller pieces in a muffin tin, or even try baking it free-form. The thing about babka is that even if it isn't perfect in your eyes, when it comes out of the oven hot and fragrant, your friends and family will still devour it.

½ teaspoon vanilla extract

120 grams (½ cup) whole milk (at room temperature), plus extra as needed

20 grams (2½ tablespoons) fresh yeast or 6 grams (2 teaspoons) active dry yeast

280 grams (2¼ cups) all-purpose flour (sifted, 11.7%), plus extra as needed and for dusting and kneading

220 grams (2 cups plus 2 tablespoons) pastry or cake flour (sifted, 8.5 to 9%)

2 large eggs

75 grams (⅓ cup) granulated sugar

Large pinch of fine salt

80 grams (5 tablespoons plus 1 teaspoon) unsalted butter (at room temperature)

1. Make the dough: Whisk the vanilla into the milk in the bowl of a stand mixer fitted with the dough hook. Use a fork or your fingers to lightly mix the yeast into the milk; if using active dry yeast, stir the yeast into the milk. Then, in this order, add the flours, eggs, sugar, salt, and finally the butter in small pinches.

2. Mix on the lowest speed, stopping the mixer to scrape down the sides and bottom of the bowl as needed, and to pull the dough off the hook as it accumulates there and break it apart so it mixes evenly, until the dough is well combined, about 2 minutes (it will not be smooth). If the dough is very dry, add more milk, 1 tablespoon at a time; if the dough looks wet, add more all-purpose flour, 1 tablespoon at a time, until the dough comes together. Increase the mixer speed to medium and mix until the dough is smooth and has good elasticity, 4 minutes.

3. Stretch and fold the dough: Lightly dust your work surface with flour and turn the dough out on top; lightly dust the top of the dough and the interior of a large bowl with flour. Grab the top portion of the dough and stretch it away from you, tearing the dough. Then fold it on top of the middle of the dough. Give the dough a quarter turn and repeat the stretch, tear, and fold. Continue to do this until you can stretch a small piece of dough very thin without tearing it, about 5 minutes. Then use your hands to push and pull the dough against the work surface and in a circular motion to create a nice round of dough. Set the ball in the floured bowl, cover the bowl with plastic wrap, and set it aside at room temperature for 30 minutes.

4. Chill the dough: Set the dough on a piece of plastic wrap and press it into a 1-inch-thick rectangle. Wrap the dough in plastic wrap and refrigerate it for at least 1 hour or up to 24 hours before proceeding with one of the recipes in this chapter.

> **NOTE:** If you choose to make a half recipe of the babka dough (to make only one babka—but why would you want to do such a thing?), you may need to scrape down the sides and bottom of the bowl quite often to make sure the dough mixes evenly. With a lesser quantity of ingredients in a mixer bowl, it sometimes takes more work to mix the dough. If the dough hook is not kneading the dough well (because the volume is too small), remove the dough from the bowl and stretch and fold it by hand until the dough is smooth.

Advanced Babka Dough

Makes about 1.1 kilos (2⅓ pounds) of dough, for three 9-by-2¾-by-2-inch babkas

The best babka starts with a laminated dough, meaning it has very thin layers of butter sandwiched throughout (as you'll find in croissants and puff pastry). Making a laminated dough requires a lot of extra time, work, and patience, and for that reason there is a simplified version of the babka dough. This advanced dough is for those who really want to take their babka to the next level.

It is important to note that the Advanced Babka Dough requires a baking pan that measures 9 by 2¾ by 2 inches. You can find paper loaf pans that fit these measurements in some cooking stores and in professional baking supply stores (and online, of course). If you bake the Advanced Babka Dough in a standard-size loaf pan, the middle of the babka will sink. The babka will taste just as good, but it won't look like it should.

1 recipe Basic Babka Dough (page 52)

200 grams (1 stick plus 5 tablespoons) unsalted butter (at cool room temperature)

All-purpose flour for rolling and shaping

1. Prepare the babka dough and refrigerate it as instructed on page 53. Rest the dough for 24 hours.

2. Prepare the butter: Set the butter on a large piece of parchment paper. Use a rolling pin (or your fist) to smack and whack it into a 7-by-8-inch rectangle that is between ⅛ inch and ¼ inch thick. Use a bench scraper to square off the corners and then pound as needed to fit the measurements. Set the butter aside.

3. Add the butter and make the first fold: Place the dough on a lightly floured work surface, lightly dust the top, and de-gas the dough by pressing down on it, then roll the dough into a 7-by-16-inch rectangle with a short side facing you. Place the butter on the bottom half of the dough (see the photo on page 56, top left), leaving a ¼-inch border at the bottom. Fold the top of the dough over the butter to meet the bottom edge, pull the corners so they align perfectly, and use a pastry brush to brush away any excess flour from the surface.

> **NOTE:** You want the dough to be about the same temperature as the butter. If the butter is too soft, it will seep out of the dough; if the butter is too cold, it will break into pieces rather than be pliable enough to spread into thin sheets. If the dough becomes too warm, it will begin to proof and become hard to roll out thin; if the dough is too cold, it will be too hard to roll. Work carefully and mindfully, and if either the butter or the dough starts to become too warm, cool it down in the refrigerator before continuing with the recipe.

4. Fold and chill the dough: Rotate the dough so the seam side (which was facing the bottom) is now facing to the right. Lightly flour the top and underside of the dough and roll it into a 9-by-16-inch rectangle (see the photo on the following page, top right). Use a bench scraper or a chef's knife to square off the edges (save the scraps to add to the dough). Then use your finger to mark the dough into equal thirds. Use a pastry brush to remove any excess flour from the dough. Fold the bottom up to the top mark and the top down and over to the bottom edge to create a simple fold (see the box below and the photos on the following page, bottom left and right). Try to keep the edges and corners as perfectly aligned as possible. Lightly dust the dough and the work surface again and roll the dough just enough to flatten it slightly. At this point, the dough will probably bounce back when you roll it because you have been working the gluten a lot. Now is a good time to wrap it in plastic wrap and let it rest in the refrigerator for 30 minutes. Then repeat the simple fold 2 more times, refrigerating

---

WHAT IS A SIMPLE FOLD?

When you fold a piece of dough into thirds like a business letter, it is called a simple fold. Bakers do this to create all the many flaky layers of butter and dough in a laminated dough, such as croissant, Danish, puff pastry, and babka dough. The simple fold is often repeated several times to increase the number of delicate layers in the dough.

the dough after each time. Wrap the dough in plastic wrap and refrigerate it for at least 5 hours or overnight.

> **NOTE:** If when rolling, you get a bubble in the dough, don't force the rolling pin over the dough and risk tearing it. Instead, use the tip of a paring knife to pierce the bubble so that when you roll the dough, the air can escape.

5. Roll the dough as instructed in your choice of recipe.

> **NOTE:** Because there is more butter in the Advanced Babka Dough, there is about 20% more weight of dough compared to the Basic Babka Dough. If you like, you can increase the quantity of any filling called for by 20% so the ratio of dough to filling remains in balance.

Chocolate Babka

Makes 3 babkas using the Advanced Babka Dough in 9-by-2¾-by-2-inch loaf pans, or
2 babkas using the Basic Babka Dough in standard loaf pans

In Israel, just about every schoolchild eats a lunchtime sandwich made with chocolate spread. To tap into that taste memory, this babka gets its intensely chocolate taste from Nutella. The croissant-like babka dough is loaded with Nutella and chocolate chips and then twisted into a loaf shape. There is a deep, ephemeral pleasure that results from biting into this wonderfully rich and deeply chocolaty pastry.

1 recipe Advanced Babka Dough
(page 54) or Basic Babka Dough
(page 52), chilled for 24 hours

120 grams (1½ cups) Nutella

150 grams (1 cup) semisweet
chocolate chips

SIMPLE SYRUP

160 grams (¾ cup plus 1 tablespoon)
granulated sugar

120 grams (½ cup) water

1. Roll the chilled babka dough: Unwrap the cold babka dough and set it on a lightly floured work surface (you need at least 4 feet of work space). Roll the dough into a 10-by-18-inch rectangle (it should be just a little shy of ¼ inch thick) with a long side facing you. Pull and shape the corners into a rectangle shape. (If you are using the Basic Babka Dough, see the box on page 60 for shaping instructions.)

> **NOTE:** Roll going only along the length of the dough (left to right) and not up and down the dough. The height will naturally increase as you roll the dough, and by rolling the dough in just one direction,

you're not going to stress the gluten. If the dough starts to spring back, that means it's tired. Let it rest for 5 minutes before trying again.

2. Fill and roll the dough: Spread the Nutella in an even layer over the dough, all the way to the edges. Then sprinkle the chocolate chips in an even layer over the Nutella, across the entire surface of the dough. Working from the top edge, roll the dough into a tight cylinder. As you roll it, push and pull the cylinder a little to make it even tighter. Then, holding the cylinder at the ends, lift and stretch it slightly to make it even tighter and longer.

continued

3. Twist the strips into a babka: Use a bread knife to slice the cylinder in half lengthwise so you have 2 long pieces, then set them with the chocolate layers exposed. Divide the pieces crosswise into thirds, creating 6 equal-length strips. Match the strips into groups of 2 so a smaller strip is matched with a larger strip (so you end up with 3 equal-size babkas). Overlap 1 strip on top of another to make an X, making sure the exposed chocolate part of the dough faces up; then twist the ends together like the threads on a screw so you have at least 2 twists on each side of the X. Place the shaped babka in a 9-by-2¾-by-2-inch loaf pan, exposed chocolate–side up. The dough should fill the pan by two-thirds and fit the length perfectly. Cover the pan with plastic wrap and repeat with the other pieces of dough.

> **NOTE:** Embrace the mess! Twisting the dough is a sticky process, but don't worry—after baking, even the messiest babka will still look beautiful and, more important, taste great.

4. Let the dough rise: Set the loaf pans aside in a warm, draft-free spot until the dough rises 1 to 2 inches above the rim of the pan and is very soft and jiggly to the touch, 2 to 3 hours, depending on how warm your room is.

> **NOTE:** If your room is very cold, you can speed up the rising process: Set a large bowl of hot water on the bottom of the oven, place the loaf pans on the middle oven rack, close the oven door, and let the dough rise in the oven. Just remember that your babka is in there before preheating the oven!

5. Preheat the oven to 350°F. (If you are letting the dough rise in the oven, as described in the Note, be sure to remove the loaf pans and bowl of water before preheating.)

6. Bake the babkas: Place the babkas in the oven and bake until they are dark brown and baked through, about 40 minutes; check them after 25 minutes, and if they are getting too dark, tent them loosely with a piece of parchment paper or aluminum foil.

7. Meanwhile, make the simple syrup: Combine the sugar and water in a small saucepan and bring to a boil over high heat. Reduce the heat to medium-low and simmer, stirring occasionally to dissolve the sugar. Turn off the heat and set aside the syrup to cool.

8. Brush with simple syrup: Remove the babkas from the oven and, while they are still hot, brush the surface generously with the cooled sugar syrup (the syrup makes the top of the babkas shiny and beautiful and also locks in the moisture so the cake doesn't dry out; you may not need to use all the syrup—save any extra for sweetening iced coffee or tea). Use a paring knife to separate the babkas from the pan edges and turn them out from the pan. Slice and serve warm, or cool completely in the pans before unmolding and slicing.

IF YOU ARE USING BASIC BABKA DOUGH . . .

Lightly coat 2 standard loaf pans with room-temperature unsalted butter. Roll the babka dough into a 9-by-24-inch rectangle. Continue with filling and rolling the babka into a cylinder as instructed; then divide the dough in half lengthwise and set the halves with the layers exposed. Then divide the 2 long strips in half crosswise (to get 4 strips). Continue with shaping, proofing, and baking as instructed.

FREEZING AND DEFROSTING BABKA

Babka dough can be frozen so a fresh-from-the-oven babka can be had anytime. To freeze the shaped dough, double-wrap it in plastic wrap, then in aluminum foil (and then in a resealable freezer bag if it fits). To defrost the dough, unwrap it and let it sit out at room temperature, loosely covered with a kitchen towel or in a homemade proofing box (see page 97), until it has proofed to about 1 inch above the lip of the loaf pan (the dough will take several hours to defrost, then extra time to proof depending on the warmth of your room). Then bake as instructed.

Baked babkas also freeze beautifully, so don't hesitate to wrap one or two from your batch in a double layer of plastic wrap and then aluminum foil and freeze them for up to 1 month. Leave the wrapped frozen babka at room temperature for a few hours to thaw, then remove the plastic wrap, rewrap the babka in foil, and place it in a preheated 325°F oven for 8 to 10 minutes to warm through. For the last 5 minutes in the oven, open the foil to expose the surface of the cake so it dries out just a bit.

Babka Pie

This is essentially a babka baked into a pie shape. It has a thin "crust" made of babka dough and is filled with a ring of chocolate babka. To make one pie, you'll need one 80-gram (just shy of 3-ounce) piece of Basic Babka Dough (page 52) for the crust (if you are making this with the advanced dough on page 54, remove this much of the dough before laminating with the butter), one twisted and finished (but not proofed or baked) babka, and extra Nutella and chocolate chips.

Chill the 80-gram piece of dough for at least 30 minutes; then, on a lightly floured work surface, roll it as thin as you can without tearing it. The goal should be to roll it to a 10-inch round that is about 1/16 inch thick.

Place the dough in a 9-inch pie plate, letting the excess hang over the edges. Use a fork to dock the dough, pricking holes all over the bottom. Spread 80 grams (a heaping 1/4 cup) of Nutella over the bottom of the dough and sprinkle 20 grams (a heaping 2 tablespoons) of chocolate chips over it. Stick the ends of the twisted babka together so it makes a ring shape and place it in the pie plate. Trim off the dough overhang and proof, bake, and glaze the babka as instructed on pages 59 and 60. To serve it, slice it into wedges just like a pie.

Ricotta Streusel Babka

Makes one 9-by-13-inch sheet pan of babka

Babka dough is quite versatile—you can form it into a traditional loaf (see page 52) or roll the dough to make a piecrust (see page 61) or rugelach (see page 93). Here you roll the dough into a thin sheet to make a cakey cushion for lemony sweetened ricotta and streusel. This babka looks almost like a traditional cheese coffee cake, which it more or less is. These instructions will make a very small batch of dough (which is why it gets kneaded by hand and not using a stand mixer), but if you are making another type of babka, you can always just set aside one-third of the dough to make this cheese babka.

DOUGH

45 grams (3 tablespoons) whole milk (at room temperature)

¼ teaspoon vanilla paste or ¼ teaspoon vanilla extract

10 grams (1 tablespoon) fresh yeast or 3 grams (1 teaspoon) active dry yeast

180 grams (1¾ cups) pastry flour or cake flour (sifted), plus extra for dusting and kneading

1 large egg

25 grams (2 tablespoons) granulated sugar

Pinch of fine salt

45 grams (3 tablespoons) unsalted butter (at room temperature)

STREUSEL TOPPING

75 grams (⅓ cup) granulated sugar

170 grams (1⅔ cups) pastry flour or cake flour

120 grams (8 tablespoons) unsalted butter (cold)

300 grams (1¼ cups) ricotta cheese
(preferably a thick ricotta)

75 grams (⅓ cup) sour cream

35 grams (3 tablespoons) granulated
sugar

½ vanilla bean, split, seeds scraped
out and reserved or 1 teaspoon vanilla
extract

20 grams (3 tablespoons) cornstarch

Lemon zest grated from ½ lemon

Confectioners' sugar for dusting

1. Make the dough: Combine the milk and vanilla in a large bowl. Use a fork or your fingers to lightly mix the yeast into the milk; if using active dry yeast, stir the yeast into the milk. Then, in this order, add the flour, egg, sugar, salt, and finally 30 grams (2 tablespoons) of the butter in small pinches.

2. Begin to knead the dough in the bowl, pushing it up against the sides of the bowl and folding it over on top of itself. Once the dough comes together and there aren't any flour pockets, knead it on a lightly floured work surface until it is smooth and has good elasticity, 8 to 10 minutes.

3. Round the dough and let it rise: Round the dough into a ball. Lightly flour the bowl, add the dough, cover the bowl with plastic wrap, and set it aside at room temperature for 30 minutes.

4. Chill the dough: Remove the dough from the bowl, set it on a piece of plastic wrap, and press it into a 1-inch-thick rectangle. Wrap the dough in plastic wrap and refrigerate for at least 1 hour and up to 24 hours.

5. Make the streusel: Combine the sugar and flour in a medium bowl. Add the cold butter in very small slivers and use your fingers or a dough cutter to work the butter into the dry ingredients, pressing the butter into thin bits and mixing until the mixture looks pebbly and all the butter bits are worked into the flour-sugar mixture. Cover the bowl with plastic wrap and refrigerate.

6. Make the ricotta filling: In a medium bowl, combine the ricotta, sour cream, sugar, vanilla seeds or extract, cornstarch, and lemon zest. Stir to combine, then refrigerate until you are ready to make the babka.

continued

7. Build the babka and let the babka proof: Use the remaining 15 grams (1 tablespoon) soft butter to grease a 9-by-13-inch quarter sheet pan. Set the dough on a lightly floured work surface and lightly dust the top with flour. Roll the dough into a rectangle about the same size as your sheet pan, flouring the top and underside of the dough as needed. Place the dough in the pan, stretching it out to fit into the corners and using your fingertips to press the edges into the corners and edges of the pan. Use an offset spatula to cover the dough evenly with the ricotta filling, leaving a ¼-inch border around the edges. Cover the pan with plastic wrap (or insert the pan into an unscented plastic bag; see page 97) and set it aside to rise in a warm, draft-free spot until the dough looks a little jiggly under the cheese layer, about 1 hour.

8. Preheat the oven to 325°F.

9. Sprinkle the streusel over the ricotta filling and bake the babka until the cake layer is cooked through and the streusel is just evenly golden (you don't want it to be darkly browned), turning the pan midway through baking, 16 to 18 minutes total. Remove the pan from the oven and set it aside to cool completely before dusting the babka with the confectioners' sugar, cutting it into squares, and serving.

Apple Babka

Makes 3 babkas using the Advanced Babka Dough in 9-by-2¾-by-2-inch loaf pans, or 2 babkas using the Basic Babka Dough in standard loaf pans (see the box on page 60)

In the fall, when apples are crisp and sweet, turn them into the filling for an apple babka to celebrate the Jewish New Year, Rosh Hashanah. Seasonal fresh fruit always complements babka—so you can try plums or apricots in place of the apples and make this any time of the year. Note that the babka dough must be chilled for 24 hours before you begin.

45 grams (3 tablespoons) unsalted butter (at room temperature)

100 grams (½ cup) granulated sugar

4 Golden Delicious apples, peeled, halved, cored, and sliced ⅛ inch thick

½ vanilla bean, halved lengthwise to expose the seeds

Lemon zest grated from 1 lemon

Lemon juice from 1 lemon

1 recipe Advanced Babka Dough (page 54) or Basic Babka Dough (page 52), chilled for 24 hours

All-purpose flour for rolling and shaping

EGG WASH AND TOPPING

1 large egg

1 tablespoon water

Pinch of fine salt

275 grams (2¾ cups) sliced almonds

SIMPLE SYRUP

160 grams (¾ cup plus 1 tablespoon) granulated sugar

120 grams (½ cup) water

1. Cook the apples: Melt the butter in a large skillet over medium-high heat. Once the butter has melted, add the sugar and cook, stirring occasionally, until the sugar is dissolved and beginning to caramelize, 2 to 3 minutes. Add the apples and vanilla bean and cook, stirring often, until the apples become juicy, their liquid cooks off, and the apples begin to caramelize, 8 to 10 minutes. Transfer the apples to a bowl, remove the vanilla bean, and stir in the lemon zest and juice. Set the bowl of apples aside to cool completely. (If you can, chill the apples for 30 minutes in the

refrigerator—in fact, the apple filling can be refrigerated for up to 5 days.)

2. Roll the chilled babka dough: Unwrap the cold babka dough and set it on a lightly floured work surface. Divide the dough in half, return 1 piece to the refrigerator, and roll the other piece into a 5-by-28-inch rectangle (it should be just a little shy of ¼ inch thick) with a long side facing you. Pull and shape the corners into a rectangle.

> **NOTE:** After sprinkling babka dough with the filling and making the first roll to create the cylinder, push the dough back to tighten the roll. Roll the cylinder again and push back on the dough to tighten it. This way you are compacting the cylinder so you can get more turns in it, creating more layers when the babka is sliced.

3. Fill the dough and divide it into strips: Sprinkle half the apples evenly over the dough, leaving a 1-inch border at the bottom, then roll the dough from the top down, forming a tight cylinder. Pick up the cylinder, holding one end in each hand, and gently stretch it. Using a bread knife, slice the cylinder crosswise into thirds. Repeat with the other piece of dough so you have a total of 6 filled segments.

4. Twist the strips to make the babkas: Take 2 pieces of dough, overlap one over the other to form an X, and twist the ends together like the threads on a screw so

you have at least 2 twists on each side of the X. Repeat with the remaining pieces of dough.

5. Let the babkas proof: Place each twisted babka in a prepared loaf pan. Cover the pans with a dry kitchen towel and set them aside in a warm, draft-free spot until the dough rises 1 to 2 inches above the rim of the pan and is very soft and jiggly to the touch, 1½ to 2 hours, depending on how warm your room is.

6. Preheat the oven to 350°F.

7. Bake the babkas: Make the egg wash by whisking the egg, water, and salt together in a small bowl. Brush each of the babkas with egg wash and then sprinkle them generously with the almonds. Bake until golden brown, 20 to 25 minutes, loosely tenting them with aluminum foil if they begin to get too dark.

8. Meanwhile, make the simple syrup: Combine the sugar and water in a small saucepan and bring to a boil over high heat. Reduce the heat to medium-low and simmer, stirring occasionally to dissolve the sugar. Turn off the heat and set aside the syrup to cool.

9. Remove the pans from the oven and, while the babkas are still hot, brush the tops with the simple syrup. Once the babkas are completely cooled, turn them out of the loaf pans, slice, and serve.

Poppy Seed Babka

Makes 3 babkas

The edges of these cakes stay soft and tender since they bake connected to one another, while the tops turn a deep amber color. Slice a cake open and you'll discover that it is loaded with poppy seeds. Note: It is best to make the dough the day before making this babka.

DOUGH

115 grams (½ cup) lukewarm water

45 grams (¼ cup plus 1 tablespoon) fresh yeast or 15 grams (1 tablespoon) active dry yeast

375 grams (3 cups) all-purpose flour (sifted, 11.7%), plus extra for dusting and kneading

350 grams (2¾ cups) self-rising flour (sifted)

200 grams (1 cup) granulated sugar

200 grams (1 stick plus 5 tablespoons) unsalted butter (at cool room temperature)

200 grams (¾ cup plus 2 tablespoons) sour cream

1 large egg

2 large egg yolks

30 grams (2 tablespoons) unsalted butter (at room temperature)

POPPY SEED FILLING

400 grams (3½ cups) poppy seeds (see Note on page 71)

520 grams (2¼ cups) whole milk

200 grams (1 cup) granulated sugar

30 grams (2 tablespoons) apricot jam

50 grams (¼ cup) cookie or cake crumbs (if needed; see page 73)

EGG WASH

1 large egg

1 tablespoon water

Pinch of fine salt

1. Make the dough: Pour the water into the bowl of a stand mixer fitted with the dough hook. If using fresh yeast, crumble the yeast into the bowl and use a fork or your fingers to lightly mix the yeast into the water. Sift the all-purpose flour and self-rising flour together into a bowl; if using active dry yeast, stir it into the sifted flour. Add the flour to the water, then add the sugar, cool butter, sour cream, whole egg, and egg yolks.

2. Mix the dough on low speed, scraping down the sides and bottom of the bowl as needed and pulling the dough off the hook as it accumulates there, until it is well combined, about 1 minute (it will be very sticky). Increase the speed to medium and continue to mix until the dough is soft and smooth, about 3 minutes.

3. Stretch and fold the dough, then let it rise: Generously flour your work surface (this is a very soft and sticky dough, and it's okay to use a good amount of flour to finish kneading). Use a plastic dough scraper to transfer the dough to the floured surface, then flour the top. Stretch and tear one corner of the dough, folding it on top of itself. Give the dough a quarter turn and repeat for 1 to 2 minutes, until the dough begins to resist tearing. Turn the dough over and round it into a ball. Take some flour from the work surface and use it to flour a large bowl. Add the dough to the bowl, lightly flour the top, cover the bowl with plastic wrap, and set it aside to rise until it has doubled in

volume, about 1 hour. Then refrigerate at least 3 hours or, preferably, overnight.

4. Make the filling: Put the poppy seeds in a food processor or high-powered blender and grind them until they are finely ground, stopping before they start to turn into a paste. Combine the milk and sugar in a medium saucepan, set it over medium heat, and stir often until the sugar dissolves, about 2 minutes; then stir in the ground poppy seeds. Reduce the heat to low and cook, stirring often (otherwise the poppy seeds could stick to the bottom of the pan and burn), until the mixture thickens and the poppy seeds have absorbed all the milk and the mixture begins to bubble, 6 to 7 minutes. Stir in the apricot jam and transfer the filling to a shallow bowl or baking dish. Cover the surface directly with plastic wrap and set aside at room temperature to cool completely. If there is some moisture pooling in the bowl after the poppy seed filling has cooled, stir in about ¼ cup of neutral-flavored cookie or cake crumbs (crumbled muffins and biscuits work well too) to absorb some of the moisture and lighten the filling.

NOTE: Always taste poppy seeds before using them. They should be earthy and not exceedingly bitter. Poppy seeds have a high oil content and should be stored in the freezer to keep them at optimal freshness. From the moment the poppy seeds are ground, they should be held in the refrigerator because they get oxygenated and spoil very quickly. Some spice shops (especially Indian markets or Middle Eastern shops) will actually grind the poppy seeds for you—ask if your spice shop offers this service. The poppy seeds are crushed rather than ground, which creates a nicer consistency. If you don't use the ground poppy seeds immediately, freeze them.

5. Divide the dough: Grease a 13-by-9-inch baking dish or quarter sheet pan with the room-temperature butter. Transfer the dough to a floured work surface (the dough is quite soft, so don't be afraid to use enough flour so it doesn't stick) and use a bench scraper to divide the dough into 3 equal pieces. Use a rolling pin to roll each piece into a 9-inch square, using your fingers to pull out the corners to create a nice square shape.

6. Fill and roll the dough, then let the babkas proof: Divide the poppy seed filling among the 3 dough squares, using a knife or an offset spatula to spread the filling evenly over the dough and leaving a 1-inch border at the bottom edge. Roll the dough into a cylinder, starting at the top and rolling down toward the poppy-

seed-less bottom edge. Place the cylinders seam-side down in the prepared baking dish (there won't be much space between the logs, and that's fine). Cover the logs completely with a kitchen towel and set aside in a warm, draft-free spot until the dough has proofed and is jiggly and when you press a finger into the side of the dough, the depression fills in by about halfway, about 1 hour.

7. Preheat the oven to 350°F.

8. Bake the babkas: Make the egg wash by whisking the egg, water, and salt together in a small bowl. Use a pastry brush to lightly coat the entire surface of each log with egg wash, making sure to coat the sides as well (take care not to let the egg wash pool between the logs or at the bottom of the pan). Bake until the babkas are golden brown all over and sound hollow when tapped, about 35 minutes. Remove from the oven and let cool completely in the pan before separating the babkas. Then slice and serve, or wrap in aluminum foil and freeze (either as a whole babka or halved crosswise) in a resealable freezer bag for up to 1 month. (See the box on page 60 for full defrosting instructions.)

THE MAGIC OF CRUMBS

Cake crumbs are called for in the recipes for poppy seed babka here, and for the poppy seed hamantaschen on page 98. The purpose of cake crumbs is to absorb extra moisture that any ingredient might give off during the baking process so the dough doesn't become soggy. Adding cake crumbs is a very simple trick. Of course, not every baker has cake crumbs saved in a container in the freezer, and that's okay! You can use almost anything in place of cake crumbs, as long as it is somewhat neutral in flavor—for example, you wouldn't save the crumbs from a chocolate cake to add to apple strudel. But gingerbread or lemon pound cake crumbs? Sure, why not? Muffins, biscuits, cornbread, and finely processed white or challah-type bread all work quite well. You want the crumbs to be dry so they are extra absorbent, so you can either let them sit out overnight (uncovered) or dry them in a warm oven for a bit (but not long enough to actually toast them). Place the crumbs in a resealable freezer bag and store them in the freezer.

Chocolate and Orange Confit Challah

Makes 3 loaves (2.1 kilos/4½ pounds of dough)

Once upon a time, citrus plantations existed everywhere in Israel—cultivating orange, mandarin, tangerine, grapefruit, lemon, lime, and blood orange trees. Pairing candied orange with good-quality chocolate chunks is a magical combination. This recipe replaces some of the water in the basic challah recipe (see page 19) with sour cream to yield an even richer loaf. This is more of a cake than a bread—with a cup of coffee or tea, it's a satisfying snack.

ORANGE CONFIT

235 grams (1 cup) room-temperature water

235 grams (1 heaping cup) granulated sugar

1 navel orange, thinly sliced into rounds, any seeds removed

DOUGH

300 grams (1¼ cups) cool-room-temperature water

40 grams (3 tablespoons plus 2 teaspoons) fresh yeast or 15 grams (1 tablespoon plus 1¾ teaspoons) active dry yeast

1 kilo (7 cups) all-purpose flour (sifted, 11.7%), plus extra for shaping

2 large eggs

100 grams (scant ½ cup) sour cream

100 grams (½ cup) granulated sugar

15 grams (1 tablespoon) fine salt

60 grams (4 tablespoons) unsalted butter (at room temperature), plus extra for greasing the loaf pans

340 grams (12 ounces) best-quality bittersweet chocolate, chopped into roughly ½-inch shards

EGG WASH

1 large egg

1 tablespoon water

Pinch of fine salt

1. Make the orange confit: Bring the water and sugar to a boil in a medium saucepan over high heat, stirring occasionally to dissolve the sugar. Once the sugar has dissolved, pour half the sugar syrup into a medium heat-safe bowl and set it aside. Add the orange rounds to the syrup in the saucepan and return it to a boil. Then strain that syrup into a second bowl, leaving the orange slices in the pan, and discard the syrup (it will be bitter). Return the syrup from the first bowl to the saucepan and bring it to a simmer. Reduce the heat to medium-low and simmer gently, swirling the orange slices occasionally, until the mixture is as thick as marmalade, 10 to 12 minutes. Strain the confit through a fine-mesh sieve set over a small bowl; save any remaining syrup (see Note on page 78).

2. Make the dough: Pour the water into the bowl of a stand mixer fitted with the dough hook. Crumble the yeast into the water and use your fingers to rub and dissolve it; if using active dry yeast, whisk the yeast into the water. Add the flour, eggs, sour cream, sugar, salt, and butter.

3. Mix the dough on low speed to combine the ingredients, stopping the mixer if the dough climbs up the hook or if you need to work in dry ingredients that have settled on the bottom of the bowl. Scrape the bottom and sides of the bowl as needed. It should take about 2 minutes for the dough to come together.

4. Increase the speed to medium and knead until a smooth dough forms, about 4 minutes. You may need to add a little water if the dough is too stiff, or a little flour if it is too slack.

5. Stretch and fold the dough: Lightly dust your work surface with a small amount of flour and use a plastic dough scraper to transfer the dough from the mixing bowl to the floured surface. Use your palms to knead/push the dough away from you in one stroke; then pinch the front portion and stretch it toward you to rip the dough slightly and fold it on top of itself. Give the dough a quarter turn and repeat the push/pinch/tear/fold process. After the fourth turn, the dough should be in a nice ball shape.

6. Chop 100 grams (about ½ cup) of the strained orange confit and set it aside (store the rest of the orange confit in the reserved syrup in an airtight container to use in other baked goods like muffins, cakes, or breads). Use a bench scraper to press a checkerboard pattern into the ball of dough—don't cut all the way through the dough, just make deep depressions. Pile the orange confit and chocolate shards on top and use the bench scraper to completely chop through the dough and fold the dough over onto itself, continuing to chop and fold to mix in the ingredients. You don't really want it well mixed—you want a very chunky dough.

NOTE: When adding nuts, dried fruits, chocolate, olives, cheese, roasted vegetables, or any "extras" to bread dough, always finish mixing and folding the dough and then, once the dough is perfect, add enough extras to measure 20% of the bread's total weight so you can really taste the added ingredients. Don't be cheap with the goodies!

7. Let the dough rise: Lightly dust a bowl with flour, add the dough, sprinkle just a little flour on top of the dough, and cover the bowl with a kitchen towel or plastic wrap. Set the bowl aside at room temperature until the dough has risen by about 70%, about 40 minutes (this will depend on how warm your room is—when the dough proofs in a warmer room, it will take less time to rise than in a cooler room).

8. Divide the dough: Gently use the dough scraper to help lift the dough out of the bowl and onto a lightly floured work surface (take care not to press out the trapped gas in the dough) and use a bench scraper or a chef's knife to divide the dough into 9 equal parts. (You can use a kitchen scale to weigh each piece if you want to be exact—they should be about 200 grams each for three 600-gram loaves plus a couple of small rolls. If you don't want rolls, just make the loaves a little larger; you can also follow the method on page 20 to shape

the remaining dough into a traditional braided challah if you only have 1 loaf pan.)

9. Shape the dough: Line three 9-by-5-inch loaf pans with parchment paper and grease with some butter. On your work surface, fold the corners of a piece of dough up and onto the middle, then turn the dough over to create a roughly shaped ball. Repeat with the other pieces of dough. Return to the first piece and use a cupped hand to push and pull the dough in a circular motion to create a nicely shaped ball that is closed on the bottom. Repeat with the remaining pieces of dough (even the small ones, if making rolls). Set 3 balls into each loaf pan and cover them with plastic wrap. Set aside in a warm, draft-free spot to rise until the balls have nearly doubled in volume, 35 to 40 minutes.

10. Test the dough: Once the dough has risen, do the press test: Press your finger lightly into the dough, remove it, and see if the depression fills in by half. If the depression fills back in, the dough needs more time to rise.

11. Preheat the oven to 425°F.

12. Bake the loaves: Make the egg wash by whisking the egg, water, and salt together in a small bowl. Gently brush the entire surface of the loaves with the egg wash. Bake the loaves for 15 minutes, turn the pans, and continue to bake until they are golden brown, about 10 minutes longer. Remove the pans from the oven and set aside to cool. Then use a paring knife to separate each loaf from the pan, turn the loaf out, slice into pieces, and serve.

NOTES: You will have enough dough for 3 loaves, so you will need 3 loaf pans. Or you can make I loaf and follow the instructions on page 20 to make a braided challah (or two).

Reserve any remaining orange syrup for brushing over babka and other sweet breads to finish them after they come out of the oven. It's also delicious in hot tea.

FREEZING CHALLAH

If you freeze one (or more) of the baked loaves, double-wrap the baked challah in plastic wrap and then in aluminum foil and place the loaf in a resealable gallon-sized freezer bag. When you want to serve the challah, remove the plastic wrap layer, rewrap in foil, and heat it at 300°F until the bread is warmed throughout, removing the foil for the last 1 or 2 minutes to crisp the crust.

Marzipan Challah

Makes 3 loaves (1½ kilos/3⅓ pounds of dough)

Think of marzipan challah as a cross between an almond croissant and a loaf of challah. Marzipan is a kind of almond paste; it is very important that you buy the best-quality marzipan you can find—and not the kind that comes in a can, which is too loose for this recipe. You may be able to buy marzipan "candy bars," or go to a professional pastry shop and buy marzipan there. See the box on page 83 for instructions if you want to make just one marzipan challah loaf instead of the three called for here.

DOUGH

320 grams (1⅓ cups) cool-room-temperature water, plus extra as needed	2 large eggs
	80 grams (⅓ cup) granulated sugar
30 grams (3 tablespoons) fresh yeast or 10 grams (2 teaspoons) active dry yeast	10 grams (2 teaspoons) fine salt
800 grams (6¼ cups) all-purpose flour (sifted, 11.7%), plus extra as needed and for shaping	60 grams (4 tablespoons) unsalted butter (at room temperature)

MARZIPAN FILLING

200 grams (7 ounces) best-quality marzipan	100 grams (7 tablespoons) unsalted butter (at room temperature)
100 grams (½ cup) granulated sugar	20 grams (3 tablespoons) all-purpose flour

---

EGG WASH AND TOPPING

1 large egg	100 grams (1¼ cups) sliced almonds (preferably with skin) or chopped hazelnuts or chopped unsalted pistachios
1 tablespoon water	
Pinch of fine salt	
	10 grams (2 teaspoons) granulated sugar

1. Make the dough: Pour the water into the bowl of a stand mixer fitted with the dough hook. Crumble the yeast into the water and use your fingers to rub and dissolve it; if using active dry yeast, whisk the yeast into the water. Add the flour, eggs, sugar, and salt. Then add the butter in 5 or 6 small pieces.

2. Mix the dough on low speed to combine the ingredients, stopping the mixer if the dough climbs up the hook or if you need to work in dry ingredients that have settled on the bottom of the bowl. Scrape the bottom and sides of the bowl as needed. It should take about 2 minutes for the dough to come together.

3. Increase the speed to medium and knead until a smooth dough forms, about 4 minutes. You may need to add a little water if the dough is too stiff, or a little flour if it is too slack.

4. Stretch and fold the dough: Lightly dust your work surface with flour and use a plastic dough scraper to transfer the dough from the mixing bowl to the floured surface. Use your palms to knead/push the dough away from you in one stroke; then stretch it toward you to rip the dough slightly. Fold it on top of itself. Give the dough a quarter turn and repeat the tear-and-fold process. After the fourth turn, the dough should be in a nice ball shape.

5. Let the dough rise: Lightly dust a bowl with flour, add the dough, sprinkle just a little flour on top of the dough, and cover the bowl with a kitchen towel or plastic wrap. Set the bowl aside at room temperature until the dough has risen by about 70%, about 40 minutes (this will depend on how warm your room is—when the dough proofs in a warmer room, it will take less time to rise than in a cooler room).

6. While the dough rises, make the marzipan filling: Place the marzipan and sugar in a large bowl and use your hands to work them together to combine. (Mixing the marzipan by hand ensures that the mixture will remain emulsified. If the mixture is overblended, which could happen if you mix the marzipan filling in a stand mixer, the fat could separate out.) Gradually add the butter, 1 tablespoon at a time, stirring between additions to fully incorporate it. Stir in the flour.

7. Divide the dough: Gently use the dough scraper to help lift the dough out of the bowl and set it onto a lightly floured work surface (take care not to press out the trapped gas in the dough), then divide the dough into 3 equal parts (you can use a kitchen scale to weigh each piece if you want to be exact). Divide each piece into 3 smaller equal parts so you end up with a total of 9 pieces.

continued

8. Shape the dough: Set a piece of dough lengthwise on a lightly floured work surface and lightly dust the top with flour. Use a rolling pin to roll the piece of dough into a 9-by-5-inch rectangle with the long side facing you. Spread a scant ¼ cup of the marzipan filling along the right-hand third of the dough. Roll the dough from right to left, enclosing the marzipan in a tight cylinder, and pinch the seam and ends shut. Repeat with the remaining pieces of dough and the remaining marzipan.

9. Return to the first cylinder of dough and use both hands to roll it back and forth into a long rope, pressing down lightly as you get to the ends of the rope so they are flattened (it is best not to have an overly floured work surface at this point since too much flour will make it hard to roll the dough into a rope). The rope should end up being 12 to 13 inches long. Repeat with the remaining cylinders of dough. Lightly flour the ropes (this allows for the strands of the braid to stay somewhat separate during baking; otherwise, they'd fuse together).

10. Pinch the ends of 3 ropes together at the top (you can place a weight on top of the ends to hold them in place) and braid the dough, lifting each piece up and over so the braid is more stacked than it is long; you also want it to be fatter and taller in the middle and more tapered at the ends. When you get to the end of the ropes and there is nothing left to braid, use your palm to press and seal the ends together, then tuck them under the challah. Repeat with the remaining 6 ropes, creating 3 braided challahs. Place 2 challahs on a parchment paper–lined rimmed sheet pan and the other challah on a separate parchment-lined sheet pan, cover with a kitchen towel (or place inside an unscented plastic bag; see page 97), and set aside in a warm, draft-free spot to rise until doubled in volume, 1½ to 2 hours.

11. Adjust the oven racks to the upper-middle and lower-middle positions and preheat the oven to 350°F.

12. Test the dough: Once the loaves have roughly doubled in volume, do the press test: Press your finger lightly into the dough, remove it, and see if the depression fills in by half. If the depression fills back in, the dough needs more time to rise.

13. Bake the loaves: Make the egg wash by whisking the egg, water, and salt together in a small bowl. Gently brush the entire surface of each loaf with egg wash, taking care not to let it pool in the creases of the braids. You want a nice thin coating. Sprinkle each loaf generously with the sliced almonds and then with the sugar.

14. Set the sheet pans in the oven and bake for 15 minutes. Rotate the bottom sheet pan to the top and the top sheet pan to the bottom (turning each sheet around as you go) and bake until the loaves are golden brown, about 10 minutes longer. Remove the loaves from the oven and set them aside to cool completely on the sheet pans.

MAKING ONE MARZIPAN CHALLAH

Using your hands, mash together 100 grams (3½ ounces) of marzipan with 65 grams (⅓ cup) of granulated sugar. Once the mixture is smooth, use your hands or a spoon to incorporate 60 grams (4 tablespoons) of room-temperature unsalted butter, 1 tablespoon at a time, and 15 grams (2 tablespoons) of all-purpose flour. Take 500 grams (1.1 pounds) of the dough and divide it into thirds. Continue the recipe from step 8 opposite to roll, fill, and shape the challah loaf.

Sticky Pull-Apart Cinnamon Challah Braid

Makes 2 loaves

You can either shape this challah like an épi (the French word used to describe the flavor of a wheat stalk, illustrating the classic "tear apart" shape), as is done here, or slice all the way through the rolled cylinder to create separate segments and then bake them (see the variation on page 87). The recipe calls for half a recipe of challah dough, so you can use the remaining dough to make two slightly smaller loaves or one full-size loaf plus a few rolls. You could also take a piece of challah dough, smear it with butter and sugar, and bake it for a quick treat.

DOUGH

½ recipe (about 1¾ pounds) challah dough (see page 19), prepared through step 5

CINNAMON-SUGAR FILLING

200 grams (1 stick plus 5 tablespoons) unsalted butter (at cool room temperature)

150 grams (¾ cup, packed) dark brown sugar

100 grams (½ cup) granulated sugar

5 grams (1 teaspoon) ground cinnamon

EGG WASH

1 large egg

1 tablespoon water

Pinch of fine salt

SIMPLE SYRUP

160 grams (¾ plus 1 tablespoon) granulated sugar

120 grams (½ cup) water

1. Once the dough has risen by 70% (after about 40 minutes, depending on how warm your room is), divide it in half and gently press each piece into a square. Wrap them individually in plastic wrap and refrigerate for 1 hour.

2. While the dough chills, make the filling: Place the butter, brown sugar, granulated sugar, and cinnamon in the bowl of a stand mixer fitted with the paddle attachment and cream the mixture on low speed until it is combined. Scrape down the bottom and sides of the bowl as needed and continue to beat until well combined without creating any volume, about 30 seconds.

3. Fill the dough: Remove 1 square of dough from the refrigerator and place it on a lightly floured work surface. Press or roll the dough into a 12-inch square, then spread ½ cup of the cinnamon-sugar filling over the left half of the dough. Fold the right side of the dough over the left so the edges meet, then use a rolling pin to roll and lightly flatten the dough. Wrap in plastic wrap and refrigerate while you repeat with the second piece of dough. Refrigerate the second piece.

4. Place the first piece of dough on the lightly floured work surface so the seam is at the top. Roll the dough into a 12-inch square. Use your hand to make 2 vertical indentations in the dough, dividing it into thirds. Spread ½ cup of the cinnamon-

sugar filling over the left-hand third of the dough. Then fold the left side over the middle, then the right side over the middle to create a simple fold (see the box on page 55). Wrap in plastic wrap and refrigerate for 1 hour. Repeat with the second piece of dough.

5. Unwrap the first piece of dough and set it on a floured surface, seam at the top. Lightly flour the top of the dough and then roll it into a 12-inch square that is about ¼ inch thick. Spread half the remaining cinnamon-sugar filling over the dough (leave a ½-inch border at the top) and then, starting at the bottom, roll the dough into a cylinder, pressing down on the seam to seal it. Repeat with the second piece of dough.

6. Shape the dough: Place the cylinders on a parchment paper–lined rimmed sheet pan. Starting at the top of one of the cylinders, use kitchen scissors to slice the dough on an angle and in 1-inch alternating intervals about three-quarters of the way through (so make your first snip on the left side on an angle, then the next snip on the right side on an angle, and leave the very bottom attached). Starting at the top, flip one piece over. Skip the next piece, then flip the next one over. Cover the sheet pan with plastic wrap and set aside in a warm, draft-free spot to rise until the cylinders have doubled in volume, 30 to 40 minutes.

7. Preheat the oven to 350°F.

8. **Bake the loaves:** Whisk the egg, water, and salt together in a small bowl and brush the egg wash over the challah loaves. Bake until they are browned, 18 to 20 minutes.

9. **Meanwhile, make the simple syrup:** Combine the sugar and water in a small saucepan and bring to a boil over high heat. Reduce the heat to medium-low and simmer, stirring occasionally to dissolve the sugar. Turn off the heat and set aside to cool. Remove the loaves from the oven and immediately brush with the simple syrup. Cool completely on the sheet pan or serve warm.

Variation

Sticky Cinnamon Challah Snails

After step 5, slice the cylinders of dough crosswise into 1-inch-wide pieces. Stretch the end piece (the tail) of each slice across one of the open sides to seal it. Arrange the rolls in a buttered muffin pan, on a parchment paper lined sheet pan (they can even be clustered in a design), or in a greased cake pan, tucked side down. Proceed with proofing, egg-washing, baking, and glazing as described above.

Sufganiyot

Makes 25 sufganiyot

These yeasty, airy fried doughnuts are a special Hanukkah treat. While doughnuts are a common morning food year-round in the United States, in Israel they are typically sold only for Hanukkah, to celebrate the miracle of the eight days of light. Unlike traditional doughnuts, sufganiyot do not have a hole in the center. They are more like a Boston cream doughnut or a *bombolone*, filled from the top with strawberry jam, chocolate, vanilla cream, or dulce de leche. **Pictured on pages 50 and 51**

30 grams (2 tablespoons) warm water

30 grams (¼ cup) fresh yeast or 12 grams (2¼ teaspoons) active dry yeast

500 grams (4 cups) all-purpose flour (sifted, 11.7%), plus extra as needed and for kneading and rolling

65 grams (¼ cup plus 1 tablespoon) granulated sugar

2 large egg yolks

1 large egg

120 grams (½ cup) warm whole milk

Pinch of grated orange zest

30 grams (2 tablespoons) fresh orange juice

15 grams (1 tablespoon) brandy (optional)

½ teaspoon fine salt

½ teaspoon vanilla extract

90 grams (6 tablespoons) unsalted butter (at room temperature)

About 1.8 liters (8 cups) vegetable oil or as needed, for frying, plus extra for greasing the pan

490 grams (1½ cups) strawberry jam

Confectioners' sugar for finishing

1. Make the dough: Pour the water into the bowl of a stand mixer. Crumble the yeast into the water and use your fingers to rub and dissolve it; if using active dry yeast, whisk the yeast into the water. Stir in 10 grams (1 tablespoon) of the flour and 5 grams (1 tablespoon) of the sugar and set aside until the mixture is bubbling, about 15 minutes.

2. Add the egg yolks, whole egg, warm milk, orange zest and juice, brandy (if using), salt, vanilla, the remaining flour, and the remaining sugar to the yeast mixture. Attach the dough hook and mix on low speed until the dough comes together, 1 to 2 minutes.

3. With the mixer running on medium speed, gradually add the butter, a pinch at a time. Continue to mix until the dough pulls away from the sides of the bowl (add a few spoons of flour if needed), is smooth and shiny, and is beginning to climb up the dough hook, about 4 minutes.

4. Stretch and fold the dough, then let it rise: Turn the dough out onto a lightly floured work surface and lightly dust the top of the dough with flour. Stretch the top piece of the dough until it tears, then fold it on top of the center. Give the dough a quarter turn and repeat, adding more flour as needed, until the dough isn't sticky, 2 to 3 minutes. Transfer the dough to a lightly floured bowl, sprinkle the top with flour, and cover the bowl with plastic wrap. Set it aside in a warm and draft-free spot until the dough has doubled in volume, about 1 hour.

5. Roll and stamp the dough: Set the dough on a lightly floured work surface and use a rolling pin to roll it into a ½-inch-thick sheet. Use a 2½-inch round cookie cutter to stamp out rounds of dough as close together as possible to minimize scraps. After pressing the cutter into the dough, twist it before pulling it out from the sheet of dough (to help strengthen the seal so the doughnut puffs nicely during frying). Gather the scraps; press them together; rest for 5 minutes, covered; and then gently reroll them to stamp out a few more sufganiyot. Discard the remaining bits of scraps.

6. Let the dough proof: Place the dough rounds on a lightly greased parchment paper–lined sheet pan and cover with a kitchen towel. Let the dough rise in a draft-free spot at room temperature until nearly doubled in volume, 40 to 50 minutes. (At this point, after rising, the dough can be refrigerated for up to 3 hours before frying.)

7. Fry the dough: Fill a large saucepan with enough oil to reach a depth of 4 inches. Heat the oil over medium-high heat until it reads 350°F on an instant-read thermometer. Start with one sufganiya and fry, turning it with a slotted spoon or frying spider, until both sides are golden, about 2 minutes. Use the spider or slotted spoon to transfer the doughnut to a paper towel–lined plate or sheet pan. Continue frying the remaining doughnuts in batches, taking care not to crowd the pan; otherwise, the oil will cool and the doughnuts will absorb more oil and become greasy. Let the doughnuts cool completely before filling them.

8. Fill the sufganiyot: Place the jam in a food processor and process until smooth. Scrape the jam into a piping bag fitted with a ¼-inch round tip and insert the tip into the top of a doughnut. Squeeze jam into the doughnut until the jam begins to ooze out of the hole at the top. Repeat with the remaining sufganiyot. Sprinkle with confectioners' sugar before serving.

Chocolate Kugelhopf

Makes one 9-inch kugelhopf

Here is what many people consider to be the original—or at least the classic—babka. The texture of this cake, baked in a fluted mold, is fine-crumbed and very different from that of the Chocolate Babka (page 57). Within the deep chocolate swirls of this cake, there is actually no hard chocolate. The filling follows the German and Austro-Hungarian cake tradition of being made solely from cocoa powder, sugar, and butter. Use the best-quality cocoa you can find. Great cocoa should smell rich and pungent!

Bake this cake in a kugelhopf pan, which is narrower and a little taller than a Bundt pan. You can also bake it in a small Bundt pan, if you must. Note that the dough is chilled for at least 8 hours before you roll and fill it.

DOUGH

100 grams (⅓ cup) whole milk

20 grams (2 tablespoons) fresh yeast or 6 grams (2 teaspoons) active dry yeast

400 grams (3 cups plus 2 tablespoons) all-purpose flour (sifted, 11.7%), plus extra for dusting and kneading

75 grams (⅓ cup) granulated sugar

10 grams (2 teaspoons) dry milk powder

5 grams (1 teaspoon) fine salt

2 large eggs

150 grams (10 tablespoons) unsalted butter (at cool room temperature), plus 45 grams (3 tablespoons) for greasing the pan

CHOCOLATE FILLING

200 grams (1 cup) granulated sugar

30 grams (¼ cup) Dutch-process cocoa powder

75 grams (5 tablespoons) unsalted butter (at room temperature)

30 grams (2 tablespoons) boiling water

GLAZE

30 grams (2 tablespoons) unsalted butter (melted)

25 grams (2 tablespoons) granulated sugar

1. **Make the dough:** Pour the milk into the bowl of a stand mixer fitted with the dough hook. Crumble the yeast into the bowl and use a fork or your fingers to lightly mix the yeast into the milk; if using active dry yeast, stir the yeast into the milk. Add the flour, sugar, milk powder, salt, and eggs. Mix on medium speed, stopping the mixer to scrape the bowl as needed, until the dough comes together in a well-mixed mass, about 2 minutes. With the mixer on medium speed, gradually add 60 grams (4 tablespoons) of the butter, a small pinch at a time, making sure each addition is incorporated before adding the next (this should take about 3 minutes). Cover the bowl with plastic wrap and set it aside at room temperature until the dough has nearly doubled in volume, about 30 minutes (depending on how warm the room is).

2. Return the bowl to the stand mixer and, while mixing on medium speed, add the remaining 90 grams (6 tablespoons) unsalted butter, a pinch at a time. Use a plastic dough scraper to transfer the dough to a large sheet of plastic wrap. Gently shape the dough into a 1-inch-thick rectangle, wrap it in plastic wrap, and refrigerate for at least 8 hours and up to 24 hours.

3. **Make the filling:** In a medium bowl, stir together the sugar, cocoa powder, and butter. Add the boiling water and stir to combine.

4. **Roll and fill the dough:** Grease the kugelhopf pan with the remaining 45 grams (3 tablespoons) butter. (The pan needs to be heavily buttered so the baked dough doesn't stick.) Place the chilled dough on a lightly floured work surface and sprinkle the top with flour. Roll the dough into a 12-inch square, lifting it and flouring as needed to ensure that the dough doesn't stick, and making sure the square is very even (square off the edges and corners of the dough with the dough scraper or a bench scraper if necessary). Use an offset spatula or a butter knife to spread the cocoa filling all the way to the top and left and right edges, leaving a 1-inch border at the bottom edge.

5. **Shape and proof the kugelhopf:** Roll the dough from the top to the bottom in a tight cylinder, pushing back on the cylinder after every roll to make it even tighter. Dab a little water along the bottom edge, roll the cylinder over onto the border, and press lightly to seal it at the seam. Open the center of one end of the roll and fit the other end inside, forming a circle; then pinch the seams shut. Carefully transfer the dough to the prepared pan, seam-side up (this is important—otherwise, the filling could leak out). Cover the pan with a dry kitchen towel and set it aside in a warm, draft-free spot until the dough has doubled in volume and is very soft and jiggly to the touch, 2 to 3 hours, depending on how warm your room is.

continued

6. Preheat the oven to 325°F.

7. Uncover the pan and bake the kugelhopf until it is golden brown on top, 40 to 45 minutes. Remove the pan from the oven and set it aside for 10 minutes before turning the kugelhopf out onto a wire rack. Then immediately add the glaze: brush the kugelhopf with the melted butter and sprinkle the sugar over the top and sides. Let it cool completely before slicing.

Chocolate Rugelach

Makes 48 rugelach

These rugelach are more of a pastry than a cookie. The babka dough is rolled very thin, then you spread the dough with Nutella and bittersweet chocolate ganache and shape the rugelach into mini croissants. The key to the success of the rugelach is for the dough to be rolled extra-thin, and since the dough is yeasted (remember, you're using babka dough), it's important to refrigerate it whenever it starts to resist your rolling pin, which will happen. A marble surface is excellent for rolling this pastry. You can get the effect of cool marble by placing a couple of bags of ice on the counter to chill it before rolling. Note that the babka dough must be chilled for 24 hours before you begin.

140 grams (½ cup plus 1 tablespoon) heavy cream

120 grams (4 ounces) bittersweet chocolate (at least 55% cacao), finely chopped

60 grams (¼ cup plus 1 tablespoon, lightly packed) dark brown sugar

30 grams (2 tablespoons) cocoa powder (sifted)

30 grams (2 tablespoons) unsalted butter (at room temperature)

120 grams (½ cup) Nutella

1 recipe Basic Babka Dough (page 52), refrigerated for 24 hours

All-purpose flour for rolling

EGG WASH

1 large egg

1 tablespoon water

Pinch of fine salt

SIMPLE SYRUP

160 grams (¾ plus 1 tablespoon) granulated sugar

120 grams (½ cup) water

1. Bring the heavy cream to a simmer in a small saucepan. Place the chocolate and dark brown sugar in a heat-safe bowl and pour the hot cream over it. Set aside for 5 minutes, then stir until smooth. Sift in the cocoa powder (yes, it is sifted twice), then stir in the butter until it's completely melted. Stir in the Nutella until the mixture is smooth and set aside until it is cooled to room temperature (this is very important).

2. Set the dough on a lightly floured work surface and roll it, flouring the top as needed, into a rectangle that is about 8 by 22 inches with the short side facing you. Smear half the chocolate mixture over the bottom two-thirds of the dough. Fold the top third of the dough over the middle, then fold the bottom third of the dough over the middle (this is called a simple fold; see the box on page 55). Wrap the dough in plastic wrap and refrigerate it for 20 minutes.

3. Lightly flour the work surface and set the dough on top with the seam of the dough facing to the right. Repeat step 2, rolling the dough out to an 8-by-22-inch rectangle and spreading the remaining chocolate mixture over the bottom two-thirds. Fold the dough again into a simple fold. Wrap the dough and refrigerate it for 30 minutes.

> **NOTE:** It is very important to chill the filled dough for exactly the amount of time directed. If the filled dough is chilled too long, when you go to roll the dough, the filling will break and the rugelach will look tiger-striped.

4. Set the dough on a lightly floured work surface with the opening facing left.

Lightly dust the top with flour and roll the dough into a 15-by-28-inch rectangle with a long side facing you. When the dough resists rolling and bounces back (and it will), cover it with a kitchen towel and let it rest for 10 minutes (if resting longer than 10 minutes, place it in the refrigerator), then try again.

5. Divide the dough lengthwise into three 5-by-28-inch strips. Following the photo at left on page 96, make a small cut in the right edge of one of the strips of dough, about 1 inch from the bottom right corner of the strip. Then, starting at that notch, make another notch every 2½ inches. Repeat on the top left edge of the strip, making the first notch at 2½ inches and repeating in 2½-inch lengths all the way down. Place a dough cutter or a chef's knife in the first notch at the bottom right edge and angle the knife up to the next notch on the left edge to make the first diagonal cut. Repeat in the other direction and continue, connecting the notches to create triangles.

6. Following the photo at right on page 96, make a small notch in the center of the wide base of each triangle. Hold a triangle in your hand and gently stretch it to elongate it. Repeat with the remaining triangles, then roll the triangles up, starting at the wide base and ending at the narrow tip. Place the rugelach, with the pointy end tucked under the dough, on parchment paper–lined sheet pans.

continued

 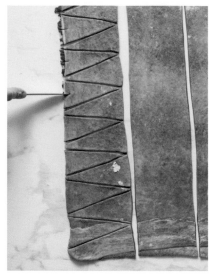

(You'll have enough rugelach to fill 2 to 3 sheets; you may need to bake the cookies in batches if you run out of sheet pans.)

7. Cover the sheet pans with kitchen towels (see the box opposite for other homemade proof box ideas) and set them aside in a warm, draft-free spot to proof until they jiggle when the sheet pan is tapped, about 1½ hours.

8. Preheat the oven to 325°F.

9. Make the egg wash by mixing the egg, water, and salt together in a small bowl. Brush each rugelach so the top is lightly coated. Bake the rugelach until they are nicely browned and cooked through, about 15 minutes (do this in batches if necessary), rotating the pan midway through baking.

10. Meanwhile, make the simple syrup: Combine the sugar and water in a saucepan and bring to a boil over high heat. Reduce the heat to medium-low and simmer, stirring occasionally to dissolve the sugar. Turn off the heat and set the syrup aside to cool. Transfer the rugelach to a wire rack set over a sheet of parchment paper and brush the still-warm rugelach with the simple syrup. Serve warm or at room temperature. Store the rugelach in an airtight container for up to 5 days.

THREE HOMEMADE PROOF BOXES

During proofing, the dough truly opens up to develop lightness and to trap as much gas as possible in the interior. It is critical at this stage to proof the dough in a somewhat humid, air-sealed environment so it doesn't dry out. To create this atmosphere, you can lightly dust the top of the dough with flour, then drape a clean kitchen towel over the dough. Professional bakeries have walk-in proofers with controlled humidity and warm temperatures to encourage consistent rising. Here are three easy ways to build your own proof box.

1. Use a garbage bag: Place one or more overturned cups at each corner of the sheet pan holding the shaped dough, then slide the sheet pan inside an unscented garbage bag. Tie the open end or tuck it under. The cups prevent the plastic from resting directly on top of the dough so that when the pan is removed, you don't risk the dough tearing.

2. Use a cardboard box: Use an X-Acto knife to remove the top portion of a large cardboard box that is big enough to hold the sheet pan and a bowl of hot water to create humidity. Carefully lower the sheet pan into the box, set the bowl of hot water inside, and slide the entire contraption into an unscented garbage bag. Tie the bag closed or tuck the open end under the box, or simply cover the top of the box with another sheet pan or other tight-fitting "lid."

3. Use the oven: Just make sure to double-check and remove the dough from the oven before preheating to bake!

Poppy Seed Hamantaschen

Makes 40 hamantaschen

In late winter around Purim time, hamantaschen floods every bakery and grocery store in Israel. But as with most things, homemade is always best. This recipe will let you make this old-fashioned cookie the right way, with a buttery and delicious shortbread-type dough and lots of goodies on the inside. When you bite into one, you should taste the poppy seeds. Because the seeds are rich, make sure to taste your poppy seeds before using them. They shouldn't taste off, sour, or bitter—if yours have been on a cupboard shelf for a long time, invest in a new batch before making the filling.

ALMOND SHORTBREAD DOUGH

230 grams (2 sticks) unsalted butter (cold)

100 grams (scant 1 cup) confectioners' sugar

50 grams (¼ cup) granulated sugar

1½ large eggs, beaten

400 grams (3 cups plus 2 tablespoons) all-purpose flour (sifted, 11.7%) or cake flour, plus extra for dusting and rolling

50 grams (½ cup) almond flour

5 grams (1 teaspoon) fine salt

POPPY SEED FILLING

220 grams (1⅔ cups) poppy seeds

315 grams (1⅓ cups) whole milk

110 grams (heaping ½ cup) granulated sugar

Lemon zest grated from 1 lemon

45 grams (3 tablespoons) unsalted butter

15 grams (1 tablespoon) apricot jam

20 grams (¼ cup) cake or muffin crumbs (see page 73)

EGG WASH

1 large egg

1 tablespoon water

Pinch of fine salt

1. Make the shortbread dough: Set the butter on a piece of parchment paper and use a rolling pin to whack it—you want to soften the butter but keep it cold. Place the smashed butter, confectioners' sugar, and granulated sugar in the bowl of a stand mixer fitted with the paddle attachment and mix on low speed until combined, about 30 seconds. Increase the speed to medium-low and beat for 30 seconds (you want the mixture to be well mixed but not airy—you don't want volume).

2. Add the beaten eggs and mix on low speed until just combined, stopping the mixer to scrape down the sides and bottom of the bowl as needed. Add the all-purpose flour, almond flour, and salt and mix just until almost combined. Turn off the mixer, remove the bowl from the mixer base, and use a plastic dough scraper to continue to fold and work the dough until it is of one consistency (finishing the dough by hand prevents overmixing and ensures that the shortbread will be very tender).

3. Transfer the dough to a large sheet of parchment paper and use plastic wrap or another sheet of parchment to press it into a 5-by-10-inch, ½-inch-thick rectangle. Leaving the plastic wrap (or parchment) on top, refrigerate the dough for 1 hour (the dough can be refrigerated for up to 5 days before using or frozen for up to 1 month).

4. Make the poppy seed filling: Pour the poppy seeds into a food processor and grind them until they are almost finely ground, stopping before they start to turn into a paste (or grind them in batches in a spice grinder or coffee mill). Pour the milk and sugar into a medium saucepan, set it over medium heat, and stir often until the sugar dissolves, about 2 minutes; then stir in the ground poppy seeds, grated lemon zest, and butter. Reduce the heat to low and cook, stirring continuously (otherwise the poppy seeds could stick to the bottom of the pan and burn), until the mixture thickens and the poppy seeds have absorbed all of the milk and sugar mixture and it starts to bubble, about 5 minutes. Immediately remove the pan from the heat. Stir in the apricot jam and the cake crumbs, transfer the filling to a shallow bowl or baking dish, cover the surface directly with plastic wrap, and set it aside (or refrigerate) to cool completely.

5. Set the dough on a lightly floured work surface. Lightly flour the top, then roll the dough into an 18-inch square that is ⅛ inch thick. As you roll it, move the dough often, flouring the top and underside lightly so it doesn't stick to the work surface or rolling pin. If the dough becomes warm and starts to stick or become difficult to work with, slide it onto a sheet pan and refrigerate it until it becomes firm again—about 20 minutes should do it (if the dough is too thin to

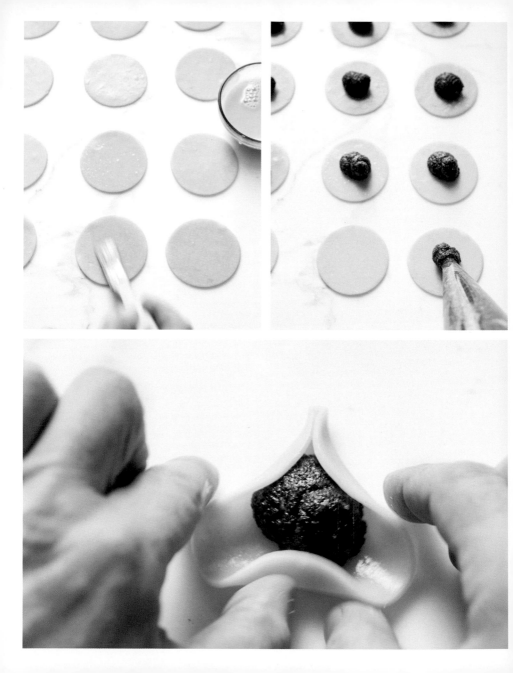

move easily, then cut out the circles in step 6, transfer them to the prepared baking sheet, and chill them before filling).

6. Make the egg wash: In a small bowl, whisk the egg, water, and salt together. Brush off the dough to remove any excess flour and then use a 3-inch round cookie cutter (or an upside-down glass) to stamp out as many rounds as possible, leaving as little space between them as possible so you don't end up with lots of scraps. Divide the rounds between 2 parchment paper–lined sheet pans, setting them about 1½ inches apart. Gather the scraps and lightly press them together into a ball (don't knead the dough—just firmly press it), flatten the ball, wrap it in plastic wrap, and set it aside in the refrigerator for 10 minutes. Use a pastry brush to brush the entire surface of each shortbread round with egg wash. Using a spoon or a piping bag, place 1 tablespoon (about 15 grams) of the poppy seed filling on the center of each round. Be sparing with the filling for the first few as you get the hang of shaping the hamantaschen—if too much filling is used, the cookie can

be difficult to shape. Follow the bottom photo opposite to pinch the dough into the classic triangular hamantaschen shape around the filling.

7. Flour the work surface and roll out the ball of scraps. Repeat the stamping, filling, and shaping process, refrigerating the dough for 15 to 20 minutes if it becomes too sticky to work with. Discard any remaining dough scraps, add the shaped cookies to the others on the sheet pans, and refrigerate the hamantaschen for at least 30 minutes or overnight.

8. Adjust the oven racks to the upper-middle and lower-middle positions. Preheat the oven to 350°F.

9. Bake a sheet of hamantaschen on each oven rack for 6 minutes; then rotate the top sheet to the bottom rack and the bottom to the top rack and bake until the pastry is evenly browned, 5 to 6 minutes. Remove the sheet pans from the oven and set the cookies aside to cool. Store the hamantaschen in an airtight container for up to 3 days.

Charoset Hamantaschen

Makes about 40 hamantaschen

Charoset is the chopped fruit and nut spread that is a part of the Passover Seder plate. It seemed natural to try the nut-filled charoset inside a hamantaschen. Ashkenazi charoset is made with apples and walnuts and honey, but the Sephardic version includes almonds, sesame seeds, dates, and spices. It makes such a good filling that this might become your new favorite hamantaschen.

25 grams (¼ cup) whole almonds (preferably with skin)

15 grams (2 tablespoons) sesame seeds

3 tablespoons water

15 grams (1 tablespoon) granulated sugar

1 Granny Smith apple, peeled, cored, and grated on the large-hole side of a box grater

20 grams (1 tablespoon) honey

50 grams (½ cup) chopped walnuts

250 grams (8 ounces) pitted Medjool dates

½ teaspoon ground cinnamon

¼ teaspoon ground cardamom

¼ teaspoon ground cloves

1 recipe Almond Shortbread dough (page 98)

All-purpose flour for rolling the dough

EGG WASH

---

1 large egg

1 tablespoon water

Pinch of fine salt

1. Place the almonds in a small or medium skillet set over medium heat and toast them, shaking the skillet often, until they are golden, 5 to 7 minutes. Transfer the almonds to a cutting board. Add the sesame seeds to the same skillet and toast them, shaking the skillet often, until they are golden brown, 3 to 4 minutes. Pour the sesame seeds into a bowl. Coarsely chop the almonds, add them to the sesame seeds, and set aside.

2. Pour the water into a large saucepan, stir in the sugar, and bring the mixture to a simmer over medium-high heat. Add the apple and honey and simmer, stirring occasionally, for 2 minutes. Add the walnuts, almonds, and sesame seeds and stir until well combined. Remove from the heat.

3. Place the dates in a medium bowl and add the apple mixture, cinnamon, cardamom, and cloves. Once the mixture is cool enough to handle, use your hands to mash it together until it is well combined. Cover the bowl with plastic wrap and refrigerate until chilled.

4. Set the shortbread dough on a lightly floured work surface. Lightly flour the top and roll the dough into an 18-inch square that is ⅛ inch thick. As you roll it, move the dough often, flouring the top and underside lightly so it doesn't stick to the work surface or rolling pin. If at any time the dough becomes warm and starts to stick or become difficult to work with, slide it onto a sheet pan and refrigerate it until it becomes firm again—about 20 minutes should do it.

5. Make the egg wash: In a small bowl, whisk the egg, water, and salt together. Use a 3-inch round cookie cutter (or an upside-down glass) to stamp out as many rounds as possible, leaving as little space between the rounds as possible so you don't end up with lots of scraps. Place the rounds on a parchment paper–lined sheet pan about 1½ inches apart and refrigerate for 10 minutes to chill them. Gather the scraps and lightly press them together into a ball (don't knead the dough—just firmly press it), flatten the ball, wrap

in plastic wrap, and set aside in the refrigerator for 10 minutes. Lightly brush the surface of each chilled pastry round with egg wash. Using a spoon or a piping bag (cut a large opening since the filling is chunky), place about 2 tablespoons (30 grams) of the charoset filling on the center of each round. Follow the bottom photo on page 100 to pinch the dough into the classic triangular hamantaschen shape around the filling.

6. Flour the work surface and roll out the ball of scraps. Repeat the stamping, filling, and shaping process, refrigerating the dough for 15 to 20 minutes if it becomes too sticky to work with. Add these hamantaschen to the others on the sheet pan. Discard any remaining dough scraps and refrigerate the hamantaschen for at least 30 minutes or overnight.

7. Adjust the oven racks to the upper-middle and lower-middle positions. Preheat the oven to 350°F.

8. Use a pastry brush to lightly brush the sides of each hamantaschen with egg wash. Bake a sheet of hamantaschen on each oven rack for 8 minutes; then rotate the top sheet to the bottom rack and the bottom to the top rack and continue to bake until the pastry is evenly browned, 5 to 7 minutes. Remove the sheet pans from the oven and set the cookies aside to cool. Store the hamantaschen in an airtight container for up to 3 days.

Date Mamoul

Makes 40 cookies

Mamoul is like the falafel of cookies, at home in Jewish kitchens and Muslim ones, served at Rosh Hashanah or Ramadan. It is a semolina cookie that is sometimes stuffed with a date paste or walnuts or pistachios. The dough surrounding the filling is shaped and pinched, or sometimes the cookie is pressed into a mold to decorate the surface with ridges and grooves. They can be domed or flat, and they keep very well for more than a week in an airtight container.

DOUGH

90 grams (6 tablespoons) hot water

60 grams (¼ cup plus ½ tablespoon) neutral oil (such as vegetable oil)

260 grams (2 cups plus 1 tablespoon) all-purpose flour (11.7%), plus extra for shaping

125 grams (¾ cup) semolina

25 grams (2 tablespoons) granulated sugar

5 grams (1¼ teaspoons) baking powder

1 vanilla bean, split, seeds scraped out and reserved

¼ teaspoon neroli oil, rose water, or orange blossom water

¼ teaspoon fine salt

105 grams (7 tablespoons) unsalted butter (at room temperature)

DATE FILLING

300 grams (1¾ lightly packed cups) pitted soft Medjool dates

20 grams (1½ tablespoons) neutral oil (such as vegetable oil), plus extra for your hands

20 grams (1 tablespoon plus 2 teaspoons) hot water

½ teaspoon ground cinnamon

¼ teaspoon ground cardamom

80 grams (heaping ¾ cup) walnuts, chopped

Confectioners' sugar for finishing

---

1. Make the mamoul dough: Pour the water and oil into the bowl of a stand mixer fitted with the paddle attachment. Add the flour, semolina, sugar, baking powder, vanilla seeds, neroli oil, and salt and mix on low speed until combined, about 30 seconds. With the mixer on medium-low speed, begin to add the

butter, 1 tablespoon at a time, waiting a few seconds before adding the next bit of butter. Continue to mix the dough until it is smooth and of one consistency.

2. Transfer the dough to a large sheet of plastic wrap and press it into a rectangle about 1 inch thick. Wrap the dough well in the plastic wrap and refrigerate for 2 hours.

3. While the dough chills, make the date filling: Place the dates, oil, hot water, cinnamon, and cardamom in a medium saucepan and stir over medium-low heat until the mixture is sticky and jammy. Add the walnuts and stir to combine, then transfer the mixture to a bowl and set it aside to cool.

4. Pour a few tablespoons of oil into a small bowl and use it to lightly grease your hands. Scoop up a large-marble-size portion of the date mixture and roll it between your palms into a ball. Repeat; you should end up with about 40 date balls.

5. Unwrap the dough and place it on a lightly floured work surface. Divide the dough lengthwise into 4 equal strips, then cut each strip crosswise into 10 equal squares (you should end up with 40 pieces of dough). Roll each square of dough between your palms to form a ball, then flatten the ball into a thin disk. Place a date ball in the middle, and fold the edges of the dough around the date ball. Pinch the seams together to seal the ball and roll again to make sure the date ball is nicely enclosed. Place the mamoul on a parchment paper–lined sheet pan. Repeat with the remaining pieces of dough. Refrigerate the mamoul for 30 minutes.

6. Adjust one oven rack to the upper-middle position and another to the lower-middle position. Preheat the oven to 325°F.

7. Use a fork or a dough crimper to create a pattern on each mamoul (dip in flour each time to prevent the fork or crimper from sticking; if the dough becomes too sticky, refrigerate the balls until they are once again easy to work with), or pinch the dough to create fluted, crimped ruffles. Divide the mamoul among 2 parchment paper–lined sheet pans and bake, turning the sheets and rotating them between the bottom and top racks midway through, until the bottoms of the cookies are golden and the tops are baked but not browned at all, about 10 minutes. Remove from the oven and let the cookies cool completely on the pans before dusting them with confectioners' sugar.

Coconut Macaroons

Makes 48 macaroons

Flour-free and Passover-friendly, these macaroons are a holiday favorite.

4 large egg whites (120 grams/ about ½ cup)

230 grams (1 cup plus 2 tablespoons) granulated sugar

210 grams (2½ packed cups) desiccated unsweetened coconut

30 grams (2 tablespoons) apricot jam

1. Pour enough water into a medium saucepan to reach a depth of 2 inches and bring it to a simmer over medium heat. In a heat-safe medium bowl, whisk the egg whites and sugar together. Reduce the heat under the saucepan to low and set the bowl of egg whites on top. Heat the egg whites, whisking continuously, until the sugar is dissolved.

2. Remove the bowl from the saucepan and stir in the coconut and apricot jam. Cover the mixture directly with plastic wrap and refrigerate for 30 minutes.

3. Adjust one oven rack to the upper-middle position and another to the lower-middle position. Preheat the oven to 450°F.

4. Line 2 rimmed sheet pans with parchment paper. Take a scant 1 tablespoon (11 to 12 grams) of the coconut mixture and shape it into

a small ball. Place the ball on one of the prepared sheet pans and flatten it out as even as possible (wet your fingers to keep the mixture from sticking). Repeat until the sheet pan is full; then repeat the process with the remaining dough on the other prepared sheet pan. If there are a lot of cracks around the edges of the macaroons, use a wet finger to patch and smooth the edges.

5. Bake the macaroons, rotating the sheets between the top and bottom racks midway through baking, until they are golden brown, 4 to 6 minutes total. Remove the pans from the oven, and let the macaroons cool completely on the sheets. Then serve them or store them in an airtight container for up to 3 days. (The macaroons can also be frozen on the sheet pans and then transferred to a resealable plastic freezer bag and frozen for up to 1 month.)

INDEX

CONVERSION CHARTS

Here are rounded-off equivalents between the metric system and the traditional systems that are used in the United States to measure weight and volume.

FRACTIONS	DECIMALS
1/8	.125
1/4	.25
1/3	.33
3/8	.375
1/2	.5
5/8	.625
2/3	.67
3/4	.75
7/8	.875

WEIGHTS

US/UK	METRIC
1/4 oz	7 g
1/2 oz	15 g
1 oz	30 g
2 oz	55 g
3 oz	85 g
4 oz	110 g
5 oz	140 g
6 oz	170 g
7 oz	200 g
8 oz (1/2 lb)	225 g
9 oz	250 g
10 oz	280 g
11 oz	310 g
12 oz	340 g
13 oz	370 g
14 oz	400 g
15 oz	425 g
16 oz (1 lb)	455 g

VOLUME

AMERICAN	IMPERIAL	METRIC
1/4 tsp		1.25 ml
1/2 tsp		2.5 ml
1 tsp		5 ml
1/2 Tbsp (1 1/2 tsp)		7.5 ml
1 Tbsp (3 tsp)		15 ml
1/4 cup (4 Tbsp)	2 fl oz	60 ml
1/3 cup (5 Tbsp)	2 1/2 fl oz	75 ml
1/2 cup (8 Tbsp)	4 fl oz	125 ml
2/3 cup (10 Tbsp)	5 fl oz	150 ml
3/4 cup (12 Tbsp)	6 fl oz	175 ml
1 cup (16 Tbsp)	8 fl oz	250 ml
1 1/4 cups	10 fl oz	300 ml
1 1/2 cups	12 fl oz	350 ml
2 cups (1 pint)	16 fl oz	500 ml
2 1/2 cups	20 fl oz (1 pint)	625 ml
5 cups	40 fl oz (1 qt)	1.25 l

OVEN TEMPERATURES

	°F	°C	GAS MARK
very cool	250-275	130-140	1/2-1
cool	300	148	2
warm	325	163	3
moderate	350	177	4
moderately hot	375-400	190-204	5-6
hot	425	218	7
very hot	450-475	232-245	8-9

°C/F TO °F/C CONVERSION CHART

°C/F	°C	°F	°C/F	°C	°F	°C/F	°C	°F	°C/F	°C	°F
90	32	194	220	104	428	350	177	662	480	249	896
100	38	212	230	110	446	360	182	680	490	254	914
110	43	230	240	116	464	370	188	698	500	260	932
120	49	248	250	121	482	380	193	716	510	266	950
130	54	266	260	127	500	390	199	734	520	271	968
140	60	284	270	132	518	400	204	752	530	277	986
150	66	302	280	138	536	410	210	770	540	282	1,004
160	71	320	290	143	554	420	216	788	550	288	1,022
170	77	338	300	149	572	430	221	806			
180	82	356	310	154	590	440	227	824			
190	88	374	320	160	608	450	232	842			
200	93	392	330	166	626	460	238	860			
210	99	410	340	171	644	470	243	878			

Example: If your temperature is 90°F, your conversion is 32°C; if your temperature is 90°C, your conversion is 194°F.

Library of Congress Cataloging-in-Publication Data

Names: Scheft, Uri, author.
Title: The Artisanal kitchen: Jewish holiday baking : inspired recipes for
    Rosh Hashanah, Hanukkah, Purim, Passover, and more / Uri Scheft.
Description: New York City : Artisan, a division of Workman
    Publishing Co., Inc., 2020. | Includes index.
Identifiers: LCCN 2019048611 | ISBN 9781579659615 (hardcover)
Subjects: LCSH: Baking. | Holiday cooking. | Jewish cooking. | Fasts and
    feasts—Judaism. | LCGFT: Cookbooks.
Classification: LCC TX724 .S32 2020 | DDC 641.5/676—dc23
LC record available at https://lccn.loc.gov/2019048611

Cover design by Hanh Le
Interior design by Hanh Le, adapted from an original design by Toni Tajima

Artisan books are available at special discounts when purchased in bulk for
premiums and sales promotions as well as for fund-raising or educational
use. Special editions or book excerpts also can be created to specification.
For details, contact the Special Sales Director at the address below, or send
an e-mail to specialmarkets@workman.com.

For speaking engagements, contact speakersbureau@workman.com.

Published by Artisan
A division of Workman Publishing Co., Inc.
225 Varick Street
New York, NY 10014-4381
artisanbooks.com
Artisan is a registered trademark of Workman Publishing Co., Inc.

This book has been adapted from *Breaking Breads* (Artisan, 2016).

Published simultaneously in Canada by Thomas Allen & Son, Limited

Printed in China

First printing, August 2020

10 9 8 7 6 5 4 3 2 1